M000208151

I'M NEVER DRINKING AGAIN

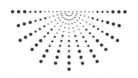

TRISH TAYLOR

I'm Never Drinking Again

by

Trish Taylor

Copyright © Trish Taylor 2018

The moral right of the author has been asserted.

All rights reserved.
No part of this publication may be reproduced, stored in a retrieval system, or transmitted, in any form or by any means, without the prior permission in writing of the author, nor be otherwise circulated in any form of binding or cover other than that in which it is published and without a similar condition including this condition being imposed on the subsequent purchaser.

For privacy reasons some names and identifying details of individuals may have been changed.

DISCLAIMER
Information in this book is not to be considered medical advice, treatment or cure, please consult your medical professional before making a change to your drinking habits. See full disclaimer in introduction section.

ISBN: 978-1-7328655-0-1

Book Cover Designer
Vanessa Mendozzi

Author Photograph
Barrett McClean

www.trishtaylorauthor.com

For Pete, Lynne and Teresa

Thank you for everything you have done for our Mum

CONTENTS

ACKNOWLEDGMENTS

Thanks to this wonderful and supportive group of people who helped me to get my ideas to the page.

Developmental Editor

Kari C. Barlow

Editing Team

Jodi Brown

Jessica Forbes

Jennifer Reeves

Marc Vallin

Motivation and Encouragement Specialist

Ged Cusack

INTRODUCTION

Have you ever said, *I'm never drinking again,* after a hangover or a particularly embarrassing incident? If you are like most of us, after the feelings subsided and some time passed, you eventually did drink again. If you have reached a point where you find yourself saying those words regularly, rather than looking back to your evening cringing, it might be time to look at your drinking.

I wrote this book because when I was wondering about my drinking, it was the book I needed and couldn't find. I'm British. I loved drinking. I honestly thought the only way you would stop me was if someone pried the wine bottle from my cold dead hands. The options seemed to be:

1. Call yourself an alcoholic and join AA.
2. Keep drinking and occasionally be what Americans call a *sloppy drunk.* (Brits call that being *drunk.* If you aren't sloppy, you just haven't had enough yet.)

Neither of these options were for me.

I began to read, research and share honest conversations about drinking habits. I found people who wanted to, or who already had made changes to their drinking. Many felt like me, they wanted to look at their drinking and didn't want to do a program or buy into the idea that they had a disease or were powerless. This book is about options and exploring your relationship with alcohol and why and how you drink.

This book is not for everyone. I mean it to be helpful, sometimes entertaining, and thought-provoking. It doesn't have an answer. Yet, it might lead you to your answer.

Drinking habits can be a continuum, it is easy to drift into a drinking problem. Though I may have always had the potential and personality for my drinking habits to become problematic, it wasn't until I was well into my forties that I started to question if my relationship with alcohol was a healthy one. And that is why you might find reading this helpful, so that you can be prepared. A change in your life, a traumatic event, or simply boredom can lead you to change the way you drink. I want you to figure that out before it becomes something that feels out of your control. If you know you have a problem with your relationship with drinking alcohol, you might have already moved on from the stage I am aiming at. If you are at the *maybe* stage, please read on.

Some books about drinking go something like this:

I drank

I did terrible things

I nearly died

I got sober

Life is good

You should do what I did

This book is different:

I drank

I loved it

I discovered it wasn't good for me

I thought about quitting

I eventually quit

I'm glad I did

Maybe you are ready to think about quitting drinking

Here are some ideas that might help you

This book is for you if any of these statements make sense regarding you and your drinking.

You have been wondering if you drink too much.

You are worried about your health.

You drink more than you used to.

You drink more regularly than you used to.

You have started drinking earlier in the day than you used to.

You think you might have become too dependent on alcohol.

You think no one else thinks you have a problem, or they have never said it to your face?

You have never been black-out drunk except that time when ...

You are tired of the hangovers that last too long.

You never thought you had a problem until recently.

You have a little voice in the back of your mind that says, "Maybe I'm drinking too much."

You have pushed that voice away.

Most people wouldn't even know you are worried about your drinking.

You haven't told anyone.

Although you think there may be friends and family who have noticed.

You have friends who drink much more than you, who don't seem worried about their drinking.

You wake up thinking, *"Maybe it's time."*

You like drinking and aren't ready to quit.

You are worried that people will judge you.

It has affected your work.

It has not affected your work yet.

You think you can stop.

You are not sure if you can stop.

You are smart enough to begin this journey knowing it is yours alone and you are going to have to figure out some of it for yourself.

You are open to help in some form.

Yet you don't want to admit you might need it.

You don't want to stop.

———

I avoid using labels. You won't find one of those *5-Easy-Ways-to-Know-If-You-Are-An-Alcoholic* tests here. If you find it helpful to label yourself, that is your choice. I believe our relationship with alcohol is more complicated than that. No one ever wakes up and regrets not drinking the night before. But many of us know what it's like to wake up and wonder, *What did I say? What did I do?* We don't all do it from the gutter or a homeless shelter. We wake in the comfort of our own beds, on our freshly laundered sheets, with our partners beside us, our children in the next room and wish we had made better choices. You might be a grandparent, a CEO, charity worker, priest, pastor, a pillar of the community. Yet, you drink more than you want to, more than you should, more than is good for you. For some of us, it is spoiling the best part of our lives.

You might not approve of this book

There is a lot of judgment around drinking and choosing to quit. And there is a particular group of people I have encountered who will not approve of this book. They think the answer is to tell people to "go to a meeting" and that Alcoholics Anonymous is the only method that works. Though many find AA helpful and even life-saving, it is only one of many methods to help with stopping drinking. One size does not fit all. I also do not believe in the concept of our powerlessness. I believe we are all powerful. We are all complex and unique people, and not everyone will find the answers they need in AA. Although many treatment centers use the disease model and twelve-step programs as their preferred and sometimes sole solution it still does not make it the only option. If AA changed or saved your life, you will advocate that as the answer for others. My concern is that much as AA might save many, there are also those who are so against the model they might not seek any help or behavior change if they are not offered alternatives.

So let me be clear—this book is not about a program. I will include a range of suggestions of where you can get support in the resources section though they are not recommendations.

This book does not include a prescription or a cure. It is an exploration, the beginning. I hope you find it helpful and that it leads you to a decision that will be good for you, your family, your health, and well-being.

So who else is it not for?

I'm not trying to discourage you from reading this book, but if you recognize yourself in the following list or you relate to any of the following statements, you might be somewhere else along the journey, and this book might not be right for you.

- You already firmly believe you are an alcoholic/have a serious problem with your drinking – **<u>seek medical/professional help.</u>**
- You are drinking heavily, having health issues, physical or mental symptoms, depression, or blackouts **please get help immediately.** Always check with your doctor before quitting
- You believe there are no "normal" drinkers
- You believe people are an alcoholic or not and there are no grey areas
- You believe everyone has a problem with drinking
- You think that there is only one solution to dealing with a drinking problem
- That no one is capable of moderating their drinking
- That judging people is helpful
- That shaming people is helpful
- That drinkers have to quit the way you did
- That you have to believe in God to quit
- That you must not believe in God to quit

- That you can never spend time with your drinking friends again
- That you must begin with a commitment to never drinking again right now
- That you are certain that you know the best and only way for everyone
- You need a checklist to prove that you don't have a drinking problem
- You are expecting sordid details of how I miraculously cleaned up my act and was saved from the gutter
- You are looking for stories about AA, the twelve-step program or a salvation story. There are plenty of those and they are not part of my story

Drinking habits are a continuum. Some of you might find that even one drink is eventually too much while others can survive to an old age drinking regularly. You cannot compare yourself to other people. Their experiences are not yours. Your body weight, height, medical history, mental health, and many other factors determine for YOU whether drinking alcohol has become or is becoming a problem. If you are looking for the answer to your questions about your drinking by comparing your situation to someone else's, it is unlikely to help. You do not have the data to make an informed comparison. We will be talking about other people's drinking for illustration, yet not as a comparison chart.

This book is for you if you wonder if your drinking is becoming a problem. You might never have told anyone, and you might be concerned that if you do, they will label you. Some people absolutely love to label themselves. If it helps to call yourself an alcoholic, drunk, soak, or piss-head, feel free, but I am not a noun. I liked drinking, and eventually I found that I didn't, or rather, it didn't like me.

I don't normally use words like addict or alcoholic. I wasn't a drunk you would have found slumped in a doorway. I didn't hit rock bottom, although again rock bottom is subjective. I never had a lost weekend.

I was on an airplane shortly after I quit drinking, and the guy behind me started telling the passenger next to him all about his drinking and his recovery story. Initially I felt the camaraderie that comes with a shared experience. I was curious and encouraged, but after a couple of hours, I felt like I needed a drink. He never stopped talking about it. It was his entire life. I know my view might be controversial. I know people need support, but seriously, if your whole life is defined by what you used to do, have you moved forward? Are you really recovering? I know plenty of people who have quit drinking, and it is in their past. They don't talk about it all the time, and they don't preach at people.

If you had told me that I needed to quit drinking before I had admitted it to myself, I wouldn't have heard you. People who know, know. So how about you? Do you know or even just wonder if it's time to quit? I had a voice in my head, conscience, unconscious mind, intuition, God? I don't know, but I definitely began to hear a voice whispering, "It's time," and when I did quit, it was kind of a relief.

I want you to be aware that quitting drinking is a big decision. For some people, it comes with its own risks. I always offer a disclaimer because **if you are a heavy drinker quitting without getting some form of medical help can kill you**. Yes, you heard me right. I am not a doctor or addiction counselor or specialist, but I know that heavy drinkers can be at risk of having serious side effects ranging from mild symptoms of withdrawal to those which can be fatal. For some people, quitting drinking needs to be done with the advice and a treatment program from a doctor or in a treatment center or facility. The reason I labor this point is that I don't know you and I don't want you to risk your life. This book is to get you thinking, to help you to come to a decision, and then to talk to someone about what to do next.

So in Summary ...

DISCLAIMER: **QUITTING ALCOHOL CAN BE DANGEROUS AND EVEN FATAL SEEK MEDICAL HELP BEFORE MAKING A CHANGE.**

I don't currently drink alcohol. I am not defined by my decision to not drink. I might drink one day, though I probably won't. I have no plans to drink in the future, and I know I won't drink today. Deciding each day not to drink is easier than saying no forever.

I don't know if you have a disease, an addiction or if you drink too much, though if you have come this far, maybe you have heard the little voice telling you that maybe now would be a good time to quit. My voice was speaking for quite a few years before I finally stopped to pay attention. Thankfully, I decided to stop before I did any serious damage to myself or anyone else. Not everyone does.

How to Use this Book as a Workbook and Create an Action Plan

At the end of each chapter you will find a **Pause and Reflect** section. Answer each question either in your head or by making notes. When you reach the **Action Plan Section** use it as a workbook and complete the answers. This will provide a good basis for your next steps.

Pause and Reflect:

- Imagine there was a book about your drinking. How would it begin?
- What would be the central theme?
- How would you like it to end?

MY DRINKING YEARS

My drinking years might have looked normal to many people, and certainly while growing up in England, I never felt they were unusual. It wasn't until I came to live in the United States that I realized the way I viewed alcohol might be a little dysfunctional. I found the demonization of alcohol by some to be unhelpful, and it made me even more resistant to looking at my drinking.

I grew up in the 1960s in a town in the north of England. If you are a movie fan and want a cinematic view, go look up "Kitchen Sink" Dramas and you'll get the picture. Most of the drinking I witnessed as a child was done in public rather than at home. My Dad was a regular social drinker at his favorite local pub and he also frequented the Working Men's club. These social clubs in the north of England are where many of us learned about drinking culture. I don't ever once remember us eating out at a restaurant as a family, yet we would go to the club on a Sunday lunchtime and on other special occasions. Clubs had special deals with the breweries, so the drinks were cheap and there was live entertainment, bingo, and sometimes a room for the children to watch TV.

My First Drink

It was seen as embarrassing and unmanly to go to the bar to buy your child a soda. Women were not welcomed at the bar, it was not ladylike. I still know women to this day who do not feel it appropriate for them to stand at a bar and order their own drink. I remember us with glasses or sometimes bottles of pop with straws and packets of crisps, so a compromise was made somewhere. Yet as soon as was decently possible, we were bought lager with a shot of blackcurrant juice or shandy—a half-and-half mixture of beer and lemonade. Going to the club was a treat. As a teenager, I was sometimes allowed to accompany my Dad to the Friday night Old Time Dancing nights, where he bought me a beer. I can only now suppose that it wasn't liberal parenting—something he could never have been accused of— but the easier option of buying me something that looked and tasted a little like a soda but carried no embarrassment with the order. Lager with a shot of sweet fruit cordial was our starter drink. You could even buy a can of lager and lime soda or shandy from the ice cream van. I never remember feeling drunk or even tipsy on our club nights, and maybe the bartender watered it down, who knows? Yet it set the precedent for alcohol being a central part of my life, the oil that greased the social wheel. No celebration was seen as complete without it. Even in times of poverty when we had little, drinking would never have been considered as something to sacrifice.

I was allowed to have parties at home with alcohol from my early teens. My Dad was overprotective of us as children and of me in particular. Probably because he delivered me into the world. On a freezing cold November day, the midwife visited my Mum to check on her progress. As was common back then I was to be born at home. According to my Dad, the midwife was in a hurry and reluctant to miss her Friday evening dance, she dismissed the idea that I was on the way and left, promising to return the next day. As someone who always feels I am late, unless I am early, it was inevitable that I would be the early bird. I guess as I grew up, my Dad still saw the four-pound-two-ounce baby he brought into the world, with all the responsibility and fear that must have come with that. He believed I was safer at home with alcohol than out on the street away from his oversight, he therefore allowed me to have alcohol at home and to have lots of friends around usually at Christmas and New Year. We continued to have house parties until I was around eighteen. It became harder to control the behavior of the guests, and they didn't always want to go home when my parents returned from their night out. By that time, I was partying in pubs and nightclubs.

Alcohol was always benign, a bringer of joy, the center of all happiness and every celebration, its presence more vital than food. In winter, it was common to find a pot of Dad's rum punch stewing on the stove top. Sliced lemons with rum and sugar was our family's go-to cold remedy.

My siblings have been working through our family home, helping to declutter after my Dad passed. They found numerous assorted glasses—beer glasses, lead cut crystal wine glasses, brandy warmers and dozens of *Babycham* glasses. This piqued my curiosity and led me to go and find the product commercial. I discovered that the champagne-style offering, in reality a sparkling pear-based drink, was the first product aimed at women and popular with working-class housewives. It promised a life of magic and sparkle depicting glamorous couples sipping it on their yacht in magical landscapes. I guess my family bought into it as these glasses were given away free with packs, and we had them in abundance.

Though I observed many different levels of drinking growing up there was only one family member who was seen as a cause for concern.

When I was around ten years old, I went to spend part of my summer vacation with my cousins who lived in a rural area. My aunt came with us. I didn't know at the time that she was being sent to "dry out," and I was part of the ruse. The family clearly knew she had a problem, and this was their version of an intervention. The plan, though well-intentioned, was not well thought out. There was no support or strategy other than getting her away from the booze. Unfortunately, myself and my cousin's own vice—our sweet tooth—was part of the plan's downfall. There were no stores or pubs close to the home that could offer temptation to a drinker. Around a mile away was a pub that had a little area at the back that served as a convenience store. During our summer adventure we walked there and bought candy. When we returned home with our sweet bounty, our aunt immediately recognized their potential, her eyes widening as she asked, "Where did you get those?" We were not privy to the plan, so we unwittingly, disclosed the location of the pub, and that was the end of her enforced sobriety.

I journeyed back with her to our hometown by train. I don't think she was well, even then. Only a few years later she succumbed to cirrhosis of the liver and died in her early forties. I remember seeing the devastation on my Dad's face after learning of the loss of his younger sister. He told me once that they wanted to name me after her but didn't want to curse me with her disease, so they gave it as my middle name. Drinking had been a problem for her for years. The family saw it and wanted to help, yet she wasn't ready to quit, and they were not equipped to help her. I know little about her early life or if there was any trigger or trauma that caused her to drink. I tell this story because I saw many variations of heavy drinking growing up, yet if the drinker was not losing everything and drinking to oblivion, they were not seen as having a problem. When we label people either as an alcoholic or a normal drinker, we do not allow for all the people in between who may not be either and still need support.

My Dad drank regularly, sometimes heavily. Yet, it was smoking that appeared to do the most damage, resulting in cancer and heart problems. He outlived his sister by more than forty years. Was her drinking a disease and his not? Towards the end of his life, I wanted him to drink. If alcohol could have eased the pain that only morphine eventually could, I would have gladly poured the glass.

I began buying my own alcohol at age sixteen when I left school. The age limit in England for drinking was eighteen, but I don't remember having any problems being served at the bar. I also worked in a bar from age seventeen. My relationship with alcohol for the next few decades was fairly typical for most Brits that I knew —a few drinks midweek and sometimes getting drunk over the weekend. I worked as a singer in bands from age nineteen, and I was around alcohol a lot, yet I didn't drink while working as I discovered that it affected my performance. My decision to sample the free cocktails at a corporate event taught me that lesson. I invented a whole new set of harmonies that my co-singer did not find harmonious in the least.

My values regarding drunk-driving are such that I never had a problem being the designated driver. I have always known where to draw the line. My drinking increased when I experienced excruciating pain every month and was eventually diagnosed with endometriosis and fibroids. I found that half a bottle of wine provided better and more enjoyable pain relief than the stuff I got from the pharmacy.

You can find many studies and discussions about the reasons that people drink. A common view is that all addiction comes from an underlying cause, often anxiety. However, some recent studies have claimed loneliness and lack of connection is also a factor. I don't believe I had one cause. It might have become problematic when I started using alcohol for pain control. Did I simply get used to that method of relief? It certainly became a dependence. I finally reached a point where I felt the craving for a drink when I didn't have pain.

Life felt less satisfying without drinking, and I looked forward to the moment when I could open a bottle and have that first drink.

I haven't been a slacker. I achieved a lot during the drinking years. I always wanted to prove I could do more than was expected of me. Though I left school at sixteen with few qualifications, I earned a degree in my late twenties and eventually gained many postgraduate and professional qualifications. I loved learning. I successfully worked part-time as a singer and a vocal coach and stayed in the same job for almost fourteen years, where I was the staff representative and helped the organization to gain quality assurance standards. I left my country and began a new life all while drinking. Just think what more I could have done if I hadn't been drinking?

Do you need the numbers? I never regularly drank much more than four glasses of wine in one sitting, usually three, though I could manage nearly a full bottle of champagne. It is not about volume. It's about the relationship, the desire, the need, sometimes the craving. It was not until the last few years before I quit that I began to consider that my drinking might not be an asset in my life. I am four feet ten inches tall and during the drinking years my weight ranged from between 105 and 125 pounds. The amount of alcohol I was drinking was not insignificant for someone of my size.

As the years rolled on, I began to long for a drink when I was bored, anxious, stressed, angry, happy, celebrating or when it was 5:00 p.m. somewhere. If I was driving or out doing a gig, it didn't seem like the night was finished until I had a couple of glasses of wine when I got home.

I romanticized alcohol. I loved drinking sangria and cocktails on vacation. Christmas was always the perfect excuse to buy expensive liquors and festive treats. I honestly could not imagine a celebration without a drink. It wasn't until I stopped drinking I realized that not everyone who opened a bottle of something for a special occasion felt the need to keep drinking it until it was all gone. And people who still had a half bottle of wine on the counter after a few days—what was up with that? That was weird. They were the ones with the problem, or so I thought.

PAUSE AND REFLECT:

- Where and when did your drinking years start?
- When did they change?
- What significant events, if any, happened?

2

HANGOVERS

Have you ever had a terrible hangover? Of course, you have. You are here. Imagine if I invited you over for dinner and offered you some delicious food, telling you it would be the best thing you would ever taste. It would make you feel good, but tomorrow you would probably feel pretty rough. You might throw up later, you might pass out, you might pee the bed, and you might feel bad for the entire day. Chances are you would decline the invitation. Yet, many of us do this every weekend. I have never actually peed the bed, but I have thrown up in it a few times. When you get really good at drinking, this seems to happen less—that's humor people, don't write me letters!

My first memorable hangover was when I left England to work at a "Holiday Camp." I am not sure there is anything quite like it in the USA. A community of vacation chalets with every type of tacky entertainment that you could imagine, and many you couldn't—these included: knobbly knees, lovely legs and glamorous grandmother competitions. Meals were served in spartan cafeteria-style restaurants, and a host of activities offered enforced fun for the whole family. I was to spend the summer working in the bars of this holiday center. I chose Scotland as it was the furthest distance where the company had a location. I was ready to leave home.

The night before I left for my adventure, I celebrated with my friends in the bar where I worked. Though I normally drank beer or cider, that night I was drinking gin. I was never a good hard liquor drinker, yet a celebration required a *proper drink*. Someone later suggested it was more fitting for me to drink whiskey as I was going to Scotland. I woke in the morning covered in my own vomit and completely unprepared for my first trip away from home and my first solo journey. It was not a direct route and required multiple train transfers with all my luggage I needed for the season. I felt dreadful, and surprisingly I received no disapproval from my parents. They took care of cleaning up my mess as this was simply another rite of passage.

The next memorable hangover that also included vomit gets even more disgusting, so feel free to skip it if you have a delicate stomach. In the 1980s, I toured Northern Germany working as a singer in a band. Though drink was freely available, we took our work seriously and didn't drink to excess. In my early twenties, drink was not a big part of my life, even though it was all around me. I did, however, have an overly optimistic notion of my ability to handle my drink. We played at Copa Cabana, a popular nightclub, and I, for whatever ridiculous reason, told the bar owner I could drink him under the table. He challenged me to a champagne-drinking competition to be done after we had played our gig. It was years later I realized that this was not actual champagne, but it was in a fancy bottle and I didn't think you could get that drunk with champagne. I mean, it's just a party drink, right? I was egged on by the staff and band members. I don't think my opponent was actually drinking his, but I was too cocky to realize I was being played. We got safely back to our lodgings. (One day I might write a book about our rooms above a brothel).

My next memory was being shaken awake by my roommate and fellow singer in the band. She had been awakened to hear me gurgling and discovered me throwing up in my sleep. She was rightfully angry and scared as she knew the dangers of the potential of choking while asleep. We were not in a hotel, but rooms provided by our agent who lived in the same building, and there was no room service or facilities for laundry. There was only one shower between our band and the other musicians roughing it on similar tours. The only thing we could think to do was put my bedding in the bottom of the shower. The following morning before we had a chance to decide what to do next, the other band members were up and about. They each in turn kicked my vomit covered sheets to the side and showered without batting an eyelid. I am not sure how I got them clean, but I know I didn't enter any more drinking competitions.

On my last party night in the United Kingdom before I moved to start a new life in the United States, I hosted a leaving dinner for sixty friends. It was held at a restaurant where I had regularly worked as a singer. The owner loved offering us tastes of delicious new menu items, and he especially wanted us to try out his fancy cocktails. I always declined as I was driving. On this night I was not driving and was definitely ready for cocktails. At the end of the evening, after a few glasses of wine with dinner, I agreed to try one of his infamous Long Island Iced Teas. For the unfamiliar, it's a cocktail with one of each of a selection of liquors. I was, as we say in England, *legless*. I was a happy, good-natured drunk, and on such a special, emotional evening, I was forgiven for my very inebriated state.

The next morning, I awoke to the hangover from hell. My head was pounding, and I felt dreadful. I had already sold my car, so my planned lunch visit to say goodbye to a friend had to be reached via public transportation. I had shipped a lot of my shoes and clothes, so I went dressed in a new pair of leather boots with spiky heels. My friend owns and manages a play gym that also has a small cafe catering to the parents while their children play on the inflatables and ball pool. The plan was that we would sit and have an early lunch before the place got busy. Unfortunately (or fortunately if you are the business owner,) it got busy really quickly. My headache and nausea had not subsided, and a few dozen squealing children was not aiding my recovery. I wanted to sit and nurse a cup of coffee until I threw up, died, or felt better. My good friend was overrun with customers demanding baked potatoes, bacon sandwiches, and sticky toffee cake, and much as I wanted to say, "Well, see you later!" I knew I couldn't. I took off my coat, rolled up my sleeves, and got stuck into serving the customers and preparing food. The hangover was bad enough, but my feet, oh my feet, were sheer AGONY. I worked for about three hours with both ends of my body crying out for mercy, and the middle dealing with the smell of food and trying not to retch. After we finally could sit down and say our goodbyes, I still had a walk and two buses to get back home. I added an extra step to my journey and stopped to buy a pair of comfortable shoes on the way home, I could not take one more step in those wretched boots. This was, of course, one of a several times I have said, "*I will never drink again.*"

I feed my friend's cats when she goes away. They are indoor cats and therefore part of the task is to clean their litter tray. On one visit I remember the misery of doing this with a hangover. I am grateful that I will never again have to inhale the smell of cat poo and pee-soaked cat litter, (odor-free cat litter is a big fat lie!) with a pounding head and the sour nauseous stomach of the morning after the night before.

The last hangover I had all but ruined what should have been a fabulous weekend in New Orleans. I was not the only one of our group suffering. If there is one thing worse than dealing with your own vomit, it is stepping into someone else's when walking barefoot in the dark to use the bathroom.

PAUSE AND REFLECT:

- What was your worst hangover?
- What did you lose or gain from this hangover?
- Think of an event that you didn't enjoy because you had a hangover. Picture how it might have been without it?

3

JUSTIFICATION AND DENIAL

My justification for my drinking for many years was that I'm British. I was behaving exactly the same way every other Brit does. Other justifications included: People who don't drink are untrustworthy and spend their life spying on everyone who is drinking and having fun. I am not good at being told what to do. I have used my idea of rebellion and personal freedom to the potential detriment of my health, that is why I took so long to quit. When someone came to my home who I knew disapproved of drinking I would make sure I had a drink just to make a point that it was my home and I was going to do what I wanted. Crap! What am I going to do now to be rebellious? I'm running out of vices!

TV, Movies, and Media

Drinking can appear glamorous, as well as rebellious. The drunken poets, the wasted rock stars. What we don't realize is that those people have often gone beyond the stage of having fun. They have reached a level of dependency and can't manage without a drink. There is a seduction in the idea of drinking, in the culture, the images. Although alcohol producers in many countries often follow self-regulatory guidelines in order to advertise on TV, when we do see commercials or ads in magazines, they are usually beautiful, fit and healthy people having the time of their lives. Those images have an impact. We absorb them. No one wants to be seen as the boring one at the party. I have grown to a point where I don't care what people think about me. Is my personality determined by how drunk I am? The people who are the life and soul of the party are usually like that when they are sober too. If a party is only fun if you are drunk, chances are it's not a great party!

I am a big fan of British soap operas. Much of the drama takes place in and around the local pub where the characters meet at lunchtimes and almost every evening. Common storylines include hangovers following idiotic and hilarious drunken behavior. Many top dramas show the female hero regularly enjoying a few glasses of wine and cocktails while looking glamorous, slim and with flawless skin. Male detectives are often depicted as grumpy and flawed womanizers who uncover complex clues despite a serious whiskey habit. It can be easy to think that it's possible to drink at that level and be healthy. I remember watching the drama *The Good Wife* and wondering how the beautifully dressed, gorgeous, and talented lawyer could regularly drink oversized glasses of red wine and still be sharp as a tack the next morning to win her case. You might be saying, "It's just TV, and everyone knows it's fiction!", yet at an unconscious level we take this information and store it as fact. We are subtly influenced by behavior we see in television and movies. We watch and can't help but think, "Well, she can do it. Why can't I?"

When I trained as a career guidance counselor, we learned that some advice and guidance requests regarding career choices could be directly linked to the jobs being shown on popular TV shows. An upsurge in forensic science courses occurred after *CSI:Crime Scene Investigation* came on the air. I also received interest in marine biology after nature shows with dolphins were aired. Apparently there are now babies being named after *Game of Thrones* characters so maybe people are also requesting dragon training courses? We spend a huge amount of time watching fictional characters and we are more influenced by them than we realize.

During my thirty years of chasing every fad diet, I would sometimes spy a headline about a health-conscious celebrity and how they kept their incredible body looking so svelte. I read their "normal day's food diary," which was inevitably a green salad with grilled chicken and blah blah blah. Right. And a personal chef probably prepared it. I searched fruitlessly for someone who looked like that and ate like me. The disappointment was further magnified when they shared that they rarely drank alcohol, only having a spritzer occasionally as a treat. I would dismiss them and move on to my search for a health plan that included alcohol, chocolate, and chips. When I counted calories, I discovered that to have three glasses of wine—my perfect amount needed to create peak happiness—I had to give up almost a third of my daily calorie allowance. Yeah, I know—very healthy. Then I realized I could run it off, and that's how I ran several half marathons and still drank wine three or four times a week and stayed within my weight range. When I recorded my calorie intake digitally via an app on my phone, I discovered that it, helpfully, saved my most common food items. When MyFitnessPal says red wine is the top suggestion for your favorite food, you realize you might have a problem.

You can also find a study to justify anything. During my drinking years, I read, nodding in agreement and shared many articles that claimed red wine was good for the heart, complete abstinence was dangerous and any number of evidences that proved that drinking was actually really good for our health and it would be a mistake to quit. Of course, these studies change like the wind and we need to look at the sources and the funding organization before we swallow what they are serving up. We all have some confirmation bias, and as we have learned from the explosion and acceptance of fake news, not everything comes from reliable or untainted sources. Social media knows exactly what we want or are likely to believe and we will continue to be shown more of the same based on our biases.

I recently met a woman, through a friend, a random stranger. The subject of my having quit drinking came up. Within seconds, after she had inquired how much I used to drink, she told me how she only drank three times a week, had wine with dinner, and didn't have a problem. I found it strange and fascinating that a complete stranger felt the need to justify her drinking when no one had asked about it. I could see the cogs moving in her brain as we talked.

Since I have stopped drinking, I have noticed that my decision has sometimes caused a reaction among other people. I don't make it the first thing I tell people and only aim to discuss it if asked or if it's relevant. I don't need everyone I meet to know my life story before we know each other's names. I sometimes receive a casual question, later, when we are alone, the enquirer may share that they too have been thinking about quitting themselves. Some, like me, just quietly try out quitting for a while without telling people it is an actual plan. We might do this because we are not sure if we can quit and don't want to look like a failure. If you stop smoking, people applaud and encourage you and no one will urge you to "just have one it won't do you any harm." Because our friends and family might not want to admit that they have been pondering the same questions about their own drinking, they might be less likely to be supportive. They either:

- Think you have a problem and are happy for you (but a little embarrassed).
- Don't think you have a problem and wonder what secret behavior they have been missing.
- Don't think you have a problem because you only drink as much as they do. Uh-oh?

If I come across as a killjoy, please be mindful that I spent decades convincing myself that drinking was merely my hobby and those who didn't drink were the problem. They were miserable and missing out. And I am not suggesting that everyone should quit drinking. I have plenty of friends who, from where I am standing, look like they have a healthy relationship with alcohol. I could be wrong.

PAUSE AND REFLECT:

- When you think about your drinking, what is the first thing that springs to mind when answering this question? I would find it hard to quit drinking because of (*Think about people and situations.*)
- What other reasons or justifications are holding you back from quitting?
- Think about the drinkers you admire. Do you believe you know the full story behind their drinking?

4

WHY DO YOU DRINK AND IS IT A PROBLEM?

Once you decide that your drinking is something you need to change, you might ask a simple but profound question. *Why do I drink?* Since I quit drinking alcohol and decided against starting again, I have not come up with a satisfactory answer to this question. Other than the pain relief mentioned previously, I have no specific trauma, trigger, or loss. I don't believe that my drinking had a cause other than habit. A mixture of circumstances led me to discover that drinking alcohol was no longer a positive part of my life. Once I honestly weighed the risks against the rewards, the balance sheet was heavily weighted in favor of risk.

Most of us drink to change our state, to change the way we *feel*. When I go shopping in a mall, I often get a buzz. I can wander around and look at the clothes, shoes, and gadgets and feel different for a while. I don't seem to be able to have one glass of wine and achieve the same satisfaction I do from an afternoon of browsing or buying just one pair of shoes. I feel good when I eat ice cream, yet I rarely want to punch someone in the face, (or at the very least call them an asshole via social media), get divorced, quit my job, or kill myself after eating half a tub of pecan vanilla. Some state changers are actually game changers. Bottom line—if you say you drink only because you like the taste, stop for a moment and ask yourself if that is true.

We attempt to change the way we feel in many ways. I want you to consider this before we go any further. If you are choosing alcohol as an escape from any area of your life, then quitting drinking without getting to the root cause might have you moving on to something else that makes you feel good, or you could end up repeatedly failing. We can debate addictive personalities, yet ultimately you are here because you wonder if you drink too much or too regularly, and you are not sure if you can stop. Considered wisdom is that most addictions come from an underlying anxiety. Once you decide to quit, consider therapy or get some help to discover why your drinking became a problem. I am trained in Neuro Linguistic Programming and other alternative therapies and techniques. I can often help clients change their states and habits faster than in traditional therapy. There is more than one way to fix a problem. The basis of my belief and the premise of this book is that there is not a one-size-fits-all remedy. We are all different and we can find solutions that work best for our problem, personality, and circumstances.

Habits

When I went through a divorce, it was a stressful and strange time. I would come home to my tiny apartment—a unit in a converted mill that was ironically referred to as the "heartbreak hotel." On most evenings, I needed something to help me relax. My pre-dinner habit was to smoke a roll-up, a hand-rolled cigarette of strong tobacco without a filter. I would get a comfortable buzz, and it felt rebellious, a grown-up choice I was free to make. No husband or roommate to disapprove. I wasn't a regular smoker, and that cigarette was just my little treat. When I met my American boyfriend he sometimes brought duty-free cigarettes from the base. I guess they were all out of silk stockings—that's an old joke ask your gran. He, like me, wasn't a true smoker. Though I had smoked and given it up in the past, it usually only accompanied my drinking.

While we weren't serious smokers, we realized it had become a habit we had developed together. After we both admitted that we didn't really enjoy smoking that much—except after a few drinks—it became easier to make the decision to stop. Though tobacco is addictive, I never felt addicted. If drinking is more of a habit for you, you might have an easier time quitting.

Procrastination, avoidance, and resistance

Sometimes we drink because we don't want to deal with something. It might not be a traumatic or stressful situation. We might simply find drinking a way of avoiding a reality or of hiding from something that we don't want to deal with. Alcohol does a great job of helping us put off today what we might never get done.

Remember, I am not focusing on how much I drank or how often. My wake-up call—OK, it was more like pressing the snooze button for a few years—was more about needing it and missing it when I couldn't have it. I don't have a dramatic drinking story, but I read many in the research for this book, and I could see some similar themes, particularly in my thinking.

I never drank and drove.

One drink was my limit.

I never went to jail because of drinking or got into serious trouble.

But I still managed to do some stupid things while drunk. I have a highly developed guilt and shame meter, and it is something I am constantly working on. I overthink and worry too much, so not being entirely in control or sure of what I said and did was enough to make me consider quitting. I have had to learn that I'm still capable of saying and doing stupid shit sober, so don't expect a personality transplant. Quitting drinking will not keep you from behaving like a dick occasionally.

Some friends and I, along with my husband, once went to a local music venue to see a band. I had a couple of glasses of wine, and I stood at the front alone trying to get a better view. We had been out for dinner earlier, and I had wine with my meal, so I was about four glasses in at that point. That is a lot of wine for me. I remember little about the evening after going to the bathroom. I could barely walk, and the bouncers told my husband he had better take me home. I had never been thrown out of a bar before. My husband was concerned for me. He said he had never seen me look like that before, and when we got home, I was frightened. I felt strange and couldn't stand unaided. The next day, waking with no hangover and not much memory, I pondered what had happened and wondered if someone had spiked my drink. I didn't tell anyone for months as I was so ashamed. I had been publicly intoxicated, looked like a fool and wasn't entirely sure what had happened. If I could honestly say I was simply drunk, I would have owned it. I had been drunk and stupid before, but never like that. If I had been sober, I would have known if someone had drugged me. It made me think hard about my relationship with alcohol. *What if I had been on my own? How would I have made it home? How could I have protected myself?* That is the problem with alcohol—it is a powerful drug that can have dangerous results.

I remember seeing a woman sprawled in the street throwing up on a night out. People were taking photos and filming her. I think of all the people who didn't get home safe because they had drugged themselves into oblivion. I am grateful that in the situations where I have not been in complete control I have always managed to get home safely and avoided danger.

PAUSE AND REFLECT:

To identify if your drinking is a problem, you have to be willing to explore some uncomfortable moments and ask yourself some painful questions. It might be difficult, but it will prove helpful in the long run.

- Think of a time when you have had strong regrets about drinking. What happened?
- Think of a time when you put yourself or someone else at risk with your drinking. What could have happened?
- Have you ever lost an evening because of drinking or been unable to remember how you behaved? What did that feel like?

5

BARGAINING

Do you ever make bargains with yourself? I was always proud that I could give up drinking for Lent, that's over forty days without a drink. As the years went on, I began the bargaining process. I had heard that some people didn't count Sundays. I thought about doing that, but it seemed like cheating and wouldn't help me prove my point. Those people who drank on Sunday—*they* were the ones with the problem. I once broke my lent fast and drank on a flight to the UK at 6:00 p.m. on Easter Eve, I justified that it was already Easter at my destination.

When not bargaining, I felt that I was beating the problem. I could avoid a hangover if I had a big glass of water by the bed to stave off the dehydration. I also once had a genius idea of taking hangover medication the night before the next morning's hangover. The flaw in my plan was that the medication was an aspirin-based fizzy remedy. I am allergic to aspirin, and I woke up without a hangover but with swollen eyes and feeling far worse with another type of toxin in my system that could have been very dangerous. When we drink, we can be creative but not always smart.

Bargains are not things that people who don't have problems with drinking normally do. I thought everybody drank like me, and again it's not necessarily about how much you drink. I drank a lot less than some people who don't have a problem. It's the how and why of my drinking rather than the how much.

Read this list and consider whether you have ever vowed any of the following:

I will only drink on weekends

I will only drink on the days I go to the gym

I will only drink with dinner

I will only drink when eating out

I will only drink when eating in

I will only drink at barbecues

I will drink only wine

I will drink only beer

I will always alternate with water

Only with mixers

When with other people

In the bath

When I have calories left of my daily allowance

When I have lost a pound

Only clear colored drinks

No more than two

Three

Four

One a day

Only two days a week

When the kids are away

When the kids are in bed

Christmas

Birthdays

Holidays

Funerals

After sex

Before sex

During ... Oh, you get the picture!

What I discovered is that people who don't have an issue with drinking or any substance, don't make bargains about them. I read somewhere that if you can drink just one drink a day and not feel the need for any more, you don't have a problem. I tried. I couldn't.

PAUSE AND REFLECT:

- What bargains have you made?
- Which worked?
- Do you bargain with other substances or habits? Why or why not?

6

THE WARNING SIGNS

After reading the previous chapter, you might wonder if you have a problem with alcohol. Maybe you do. Maybe you don't. This is a no-judgment zone, and reading this book is part of your journey. I knew deep inside that something about the way I drank wasn't right. So look at this list and ask yourself if any of these thoughts resonate.

You don't have to make a note or use it as a checklist—just read through it with honesty. Let yourself begin to ask the question. I just want to get you thinking, to put into your conscious awareness the thing that might already be processing at an unconscious level.

Possible warning signs of a drinking problem:

- You wonder if you are drinking too much
- You know you are drinking too much and don't know how to stop
- You are wondering if you should moderate your drinking
- You have tried to quit and failed
- You can't just have one drink

- You regularly do things that make you feel guilty, embarrassed, or ashamed when drinking
- You have gaps in your memory
- You have tried to cut down but always end up drinking the same amount or more
- Your friends and family are concerned about your drinking
- You have health problems associated with drinking
- You drink and drive
- You worry if you go somewhere that you won't be able to get a drink
- You drink in secret
- You lie about how much you drink
- You justify your need to drink
- You justify that you can go long periods without drinking
- You get angry when people comment on your drinking
- You plan your weekends around drinking

Is there anything in your life you would do if you didn't drink? Think about the times when you have not attended an event or done something because of how it would affect your ability to drink, or how you might have felt that others felt about you? I kept getting warning signs. Regret, fear, worry—these were the internal processes taking place, my unconscious mind doing its protective work. Then it was the external triggers and warnings—a random article I came across at the hair salon, the podcaster talking about alcohol being a distraction to goals. All of these added up to the conviction I needed to rethink my drinking.

Memory Lapses, Slurry Speech

In the years before I stopped drinking, I often considered quitting, then I would get scared that I could never drink again, and I would dismiss the whole idea. No way was I ever going to become one of those people droning on about *sobriety*. Thankfully, you don't have to become a different person. I was stuck on the notion that drinking was part of my personality. I questioned that belief when drinking affected my ability to link my brain to my speech. I remember sitting in a car being driven somewhere by some poor unfortunate designated driver. I had an extremely important point to make or a story to tell, and my mind knew the words, but my lips were moving in a strange way, and the sounds coming out were like someone had filled my mouth with slippery rubber bands. If only I could get them all to the side of my cheek, I could get on with the important speech I was making.

I was more hopeless at arguing while drunk than I am sober, and I'm not great at it without a drink either. I could formulate an argument of a hot-button issue and get emotional and angry about it. In the middle of the argument, I would remember I was angry, but I couldn't for the life of me remember what the heck I was talking about. I would easily lose my train of thought, desperately searching my brain for context, words, and meaning. It was frustrating.

One of the scariest things I did while drunk was to entertain suicidal thoughts. Like many of us, I have had dark days, However, I have never reached the point of wanting to end it all while sober. During some of my drunken nights after arguments where I felt deeply wounded, I seriously (as serious as you can be when you are drunk) contemplated suicide. There is a sad irony that the drug we turn to, to quell our restless emotions can stir them up so much that we go to a dark place. It wasn't a regular occurrence, but I can remember two specific instances where after wallowing in drunken self-pity, I had these types of thoughts. I considered putting an end to my misery as an I'll-show-them to the person I had just been arguing with. I would wake up the next morning realizing that I had toyed with such dangerous thoughts before passing out in a pitiful stupor. See, I promised you there wouldn't be any big dramatic reveals, but there could have been, and that is why I am writing this for you.

PAUSE AND REFLECT:

- Is your drinking a problem?
- Has your behavior around drinking ever hurt anyone?
- How did that feel?
- What were the consequences?
- If you were to know, on a scale of 1 to 10 how much of a problem is it? (1 being no problem at all and 10 being the worst it could possibly be.) Why not write that number down somewhere? You don't have to tell anyone else or make a decision. Just answer the question honestly and give it a number.

7

QUITTING IS WORTH CONSIDERING

When I visited the doctor shortly after I quit drinking, he asked the usual question about whether I was "using" alcohol. Before I quit, that question would infuriate me. I didn't "use" I just liked to have a drink. This time I was happy to say I didn't, and the doctor and I talked about it. He was a smart guy I liked a lot. He respected my desire to have a more natural approach to my health, and we had good conversations whenever I visited. He told me that he was glad to learn that I had quit and said he often tried to figure out if his patients were drinkers before he asked them any questions. He said most times he could tell how much they were drinking just by looking at them. If that seems judgmental, I guess it is, he was judging based on what he saw on a daily basis. If you are still wondering if you have a problem but have not accepted it consciously, this might annoy you or get you fired up. Just like the "using" question did me.

A recent study showed that one in twenty people die annually as a result of the harmful use of alcohol worldwide. That's over three million people. [1]

Your liver cleans out toxins from your body and that includes alcohol and why it's often recommended that you have breaks in between the days you drink. Cirrhosis of the liver can eventually happen when you don't give it a break. Your organs suffer when they don't get a break from the constant barrage of toxins. There is a reason my doctor mentioned he could often identify those who are heavy or regular drinkers. Visible cues include broken veins, flabby skin, red eyes, and many other factors that result from constant dehydration. Without alcohol in your life, you could look and feel much better. Who doesn't want to make the best of themselves and be a little more gorgeous?

You Might Lose Weight (See Doughnut Disclaimer!)

The reduction in empty calories can make a big difference to your weight. Alcohol has no real nutritional value. I remember one time when I was dieting and remembered how much sugar was in a glass of wine. Thinking about the drink like a glass of sugar helped me to limit what I drank just to save the calories. Even though I replaced my alcohol with doughnuts and ice cream for the first few months and enjoy a ginger beer or craft soda when I go out, they still do not add up to the calories that I used to consume. And it's not just calories from the booze. When I had a few glasses of wine, I also got cravings for potato chips or some other version of the munchies. That doesn't happen after a glass of cream soda.

Imagine what you could do with all those calories? If you drink three beers or three glasses of wine five times a week (and I know some of you are drinking more than that). You could save 2000 calories per week or more. Depending on your body composition, you could lose a couple a pounds a month without changing your diet or adding exercise, though once you start to see a change you might want to make other changes too. I did, and I ate whatever I wanted and still do.

You Will Have More Time

Seriously, do you notice how time seems to disappear when you drink? It's like computer time, it operates on a different continuum. It may seem like your time goes quickly because you are having so much fun. Yet some of it is because you are not really here, or there or anywhere. Your brain takes a little holiday. This is why when you first quit you might find events you previously enjoyed now seem a little dull. We'll come back to that later in the *What to Expect* chapter. Your time can also be better spent. When I drank at home I could never do anything worthwhile that involved my brain. I am now more likely to be creative in the evening and to use the time to write or embark on another pursuit. When drinking, once I consumed the first glass of wine I couldn't create anything except the occasional social media rant that I later woke up sweating about and deleted.

You Will Always Have a Designated Driver

Yes, that's you. I used to go to events where there was wine flowing and would have one, just because it was there. That one drink which would normally have little effect on me if I was trying to get a buzz, would seem to make me feel tipsy and then I dare not drive home. As anyone who has enjoyed drinking as much as I did, just having one was like the agony and the ecstasy just enough to get a taste, not enough to feel good, too much if you had to concentrate. If you decide to lay off it for good you will never have to worry about your blood alcohol level, the words "just blow into this bag" will not be met with a sinking feeling in your stomach and neither hopefully will be flashing blue lights in your rearview mirror.

.   .   .

I remember a story of someone in my old hometown in the UK. After driving home at night after a few drinks, he struck and seriously injured a pedestrian. All accounts indicated that the victim was completely incapacitated with drink and not in control of his senses or his ability to walk, but the driver, after taking a Breathalyzer test, was found to be over the limit and charged with a serious criminal offense. He might have only had two beers, but he was not in full control of the car, according to the roadside test, and was therefore guilty of a crime. Had he been sober, he might not have been held responsible for the crime or he might have prevented it from happening at all.

Mistakes are easy to make when we are sober and adding alcohol to the mix makes them even more likely. I was once evacuated from my home in the middle of the night due to someone's drunken mistake. The man in the downstairs apartment came home from the pub and in his craving for fried food set a pan of oil to heat on the stove top and promptly fell asleep. Thankfully, smoke detectors saved anyone from harm, though his kitchen didn't fare too well.

Peace of Mind

Of all the reasons that I would recommend that you consider quitting, what it will do for your mind and your growth outweighs even the physical aspects. We will talk a little later about how drinking dulls our emotions. Though you and I know that they are not dulled completely. Feelings of guilt, regret, embarrassment and shame are often a common accompaniment to a hangover. The emotions that we attempt to mask are replaced with other negative ones.

Your Relationships Will Benefit

Talking with or arguing with drunk people can be funny, it can also be infuriating. Though some people are happy drunks, most of us, as our reasoning capacity is diminished, devolve into a sub-human version of ourselves. Mean drunks are no fun to be around and can be frightening and dangerous. When you stop drinking, it is a great time to re-evaluate your relationships, you might find that you have little in common with friends other than drinking. You now have the opportunity to either deepen those relationships as you explore other activities that might not include drinking, or you might decide to take a step back, or even sever ties completely.

Your Professional Life Will Be Safer

Another upside of staying sober is knowing you will not disgrace yourself in public and risk damaging a business relationship. Though I have had political and moral arguments since quitting drinking, knowing that I was sober during these debates means I remember what I said, and that I was rational and have no regrets. On the few occasions that I had previously had too much to drink in public, I worried that I might later meet a witness to my sloppiness at a business meeting and be embarrassed. If you have ever met someone who is drunk in public who you know professionally, you will know how awkward it can be the next time you see them.

You Will Save Money

Drinking is expensive, and cabs, hotels and DUIs are too. If you go out for an expensive dinner and you drink alcohol with your meal, that could eat up thirty percent of the bill. Have you ever drunk shopped? It is a billion-dollar industry with Americans spending an average $448.00 per person in 2017, according to a study by www.finder.com. You could be one of those people opening unexpected and unwanted parcels after a night out of partying. (See the next chapter for examples of how the costs of alcohol add up!)

PAUSE AND REFLECT:

- List three ways that your life might be better without alcohol in it?
- What are some things that alcohol keeps you from accomplishing?
- Who in your life would be overjoyed if you stopped drinking?

---

1. http://www.who.int/news-room/detail/21-09-2018-harmful-use-of-alcohol-kills-more-than-3-million-people-each-year-most-of-them-men

8

DRINKING IS EXPENSIVE

Have you ever been on a cruise or flown first class or been on an all-inclusive vacation? It's the alcohol you pay extra for on cruises, and it is the alcohol that is included in the five-thousand dollars first class fare and the vacation. Drink packages are viewed as a huge perk and when you don't need or want it, you can save some money. Before I quit drinking I had found a liquor I enjoyed that was over forty dollars a bottle. That can buy something much nicer than a potential hangover.

Have you ever thought of the financial cost to you personally? Just the actual alcohol, not including cabs, hotel rooms or anything else associated with drinking? When you start to see how much money you spend, it can be eye-opening. I discovered that eating out and trips were not anywhere near as expensive as they had been once I subtracted the amount that a few beers, glasses of wine, or cocktails added to the bill.

Maybe now would be a good time to make an inventory of your drinking costs. Get a journal or notepad and make a quick list. I have no idea how much or what you drink, and it's been a while since I have bought any alcohol. I am using baseline prices to get an idea of how much you could save.

Drinking at home

First, work out what your drink is. Be honest, this is not for your doctor, your spouse or your employer, this is just for you.

What is your drink of choice?

A Bottle of Wine?

Pack of Beer?

A Bottle of Liquor?

Maybe something else?

At the time of writing, a bottle of wine in a restaurant is at least $30.00 and one from a store around $10.00. A cocktail will set you back at least $10.00. Even a beer is close to $5.00 a bottle or glass.

How many drinks per week?

1 bottle of wine average = $10.00

3 bottles per week = $30.00

Plus one pack of beer =$20.00

Total cost

$50.00 per week

$2600.00 per year

Or

5 bottles of wine per week = $50.00

1 bottle of Vodka per week = $30.00

Total cost

$80.00 per week

$4160.00 per year

Drinking at home plus eating and drinking out

3 bottles of wine per week = $30.00

1 pack of beer per week = $20.00

3 glasses of wine at a restaurant once per week = $30.00

A night out at a bar = $50.00

Total cost

$130.00 per week

$6,760.00 per year

Look at those numbers. The larger ones could cover a new car payment or a trip around the world. You might drink the finest champagne or the cheapest beer, but I will hazard a guess that whatever your drink of choice, or how regularly you're drinking, you will have a considerable amount of extra cash if you stop drinking.

PAUSE AND REFLECT:

- Think of a time when you have spent money on alcohol that you couldn't afford?
- Work out the following: How much your drinks cost. Calculate and average how much you drink in a week, month and year. Get a figure.
- Think of a bucket list item that you could spend that money on. What would it be?

9

WHAT TO EXPECT

If you decide to quit drinking you will have made a big decision. It will impact your life. Do not doubt that this thing you are considering is one of the biggest changes in your life. Most changes will be positive. In the early stages, quitting drinking—like quitting anything you have become dependent upon—will include some growing pains.

Everyone has a different journey, and yours might be completely different from mine. When I look back, I don't think quitting drinking was as hard as I thought it would be. What was different and unexpected was discovering that the physical struggle was nothing compared to the mental and emotional one. The truth that I was using alcohol as a crutch, as a way to control my emotions was a hard one. We will talk more about emotions later.

Let us talk about your mindset and your expectations. I discovered when I spent time among people who were giving up drinking, the idea that quitting will be really, really hard and that you will probably fail was common. Let me tell you a secret—there are thousands of people out there who have given up drinking and haven't struggled, who made a decision and stuck to it. They might not call themselves addicts or alcoholics, yet they realized they had an unhealthy, unhelpful, or problematic relationship and decided to quit. We always see the ones who make the news or have the dramatic stories. Yes, I also know people who sold the metaphorical family silver to fund their drinking and others who died young or tragically or both because of it. I also know people who take recreational drugs regularly and hold down high-level jobs. Don't believe the moral panic or the preachiness of any program, there is more than one way to do anything.

We get what we focus on, and you can stop drinking and choose not to label yourself–other than telling people that you don't drink. That has power in itself.

The first sober nights are often the ones where people struggle, and it is easier to say, "Screw this. I can't do it!" and have a drink. I encourage you to hang in there. When you make any change, it can seem overwhelming. If you give up anything you enjoy and consume regularly, you will initially notice how much you want it. That does eventually subside, and you get used to living without it. Our reticular activating system presents us with more of what we are thinking of. If you ever gave up smoking, you might remember that there was a time when every commercial and movie seemed to include people smoking and appearing to be really enjoying it. After a while, you stop noticing them.

Growth is Good

I discovered surprisingly that because I didn't (after the initial twenty-one days) have an end date to my quitting, it got easier. When in the past, I had done a Dry January quit or other 'fasts' with an end date, I would count down the days until I could have a drink. I could do it, yet I was really looking forward to the fast ending and enjoying my first drink. When I finally decided not to drink again, I didn't have to think about looking forward to a drink. Every single time I had previously quit drinking for a set period, the first day after resuming drinking often came with a terrible hangover. I could never go for days without a drink and then just have a couple.

It is important to find an alternative, find something else to do. Drinking is often tied in with our habits and habits can be broken. I recommend Charles Duhigg's book, *The Power of Habit,* if you want to explore more on the subject. There are suggestions at the end of this book for alternatives to drinking and dealing with cravings.

This is again why some people find a program can help. It includes a plan and a support network of people who are available and know what you are experiencing. Though you will see in the resources section that there are other options.

It's Just Not Fair!

When the euphoria of realizing that you can quit and feel okay about it wears off, you might reach this point. A period of self-pity or "it's not fairism" is common and will pass. When I first quit and read about people in their twenties pondering this question of quitting for good I felt sorry for them. At least I had my thirty years of enjoyable drinking behind me. I know that's screwy thinking. A better way of looking at it might be, those quitting early have an extra thirty years of creative productive years, years I could have spent better. It is not that I am filled with regret, yet I think I could have made smarter choices that would have put me in a better position, if I hadn't been *enjoying* myself so much.

How to Tell People

If you decide to quit there will come a time when you will want to share this with your friends and family. How you do this is up to you. I can understand why some people readily claim the alcoholic label, it is so much simpler to explain, and people usually understand what it means. You won't have many more questions after you give that as your answer. If you decide to quit drinking and do not feel that applies to you, it can be a little trickier to explain in a way that people understand.

I usually tell people that I stopped drinking because it wasn't fun anymore and wasn't good for me. Though It depends on the context. Because this is not a concrete answer, it is not always enough and might be confusing. I still have friends I don't see often, and they might ask, "Oh, so you are still not drinking?" When you first decide not to drink, you might feel awkward or embarrassed. There are ways that people get around this. If at first you don't want people to know and you are in a social setting you can order a club soda or non-alcoholic beer (not for everyone I know) or you can say:

I'm driving

I'm on medication

I have to be up early

I'm taking a break

I'm on a special diet

I'm counting calories

If people become insistent on giving you a drink, this is their problem and not yours. I would have no problem whispering in their ear, "I have my own reasons for not drinking and you are making this very difficult for me, so back off." Be careful though, in some circles, if a woman suddenly stops drinking it can only mean one thing—the potential patter of tiny feet!

If you quit after having a long-term drinking habit, you might occasionally forget that you don't drink. I know it sounds crazy, yet we can become so accustomed to reaching for a drink and in a familiar environment this could happen, I have always "remembered" just in time, or you might be inadvertently offered a drink that includes alcohol and slip up. If this happens, I suggest that you forgive yourself and move on.

Drinking Dreams

Dreaming about drinking is a common theme among people who give up. I am not referring to wistful desires to drink again. Drinking dreams usually take the form of finding yourself in a situation where you have just had a drink, or you may find yourself drinking and don't know how it happened. I usually wake up extremely relieved to discover it was only a dream. I believe these dreams are our unconscious mind's way of trying out the option and even possibly offering a warning when we are facing temptation.

If you have a setback and drink and then have to start the process again, use it as a lesson. What was the situation? Who were you with? What were you doing and what do you think led you to make the decision to drink? because it is a decision.

PAUSE AND REFLECT:

- What worries do you have around quitting?
- What kinds of situations worry you the most?
- If you quit, who are you worried about telling?
- Who will you look forward to telling?

10

MY QUITTING EXPERIENCE

For many years I found ways to convince myself that my drinking was completely normal. I had proved that I could go over forty days and nights without a drink during Lent. I admit I wasn't doing this for any deep spiritual reasons. I was proving to myself that I could go that length of time without a drink, and therefore showing I absolutely, definitely without a doubt did not have a problem. I also hoped that I would lose some weight in the process.

I had lots of warning signs, signals, messages from the universe, telling me it was time to quit. I took a break from drinking for short periods on lots of occasions to prove to myself that I could, each of these ended with me restarting drinking and each "quit" seeming to become more difficult. In 2015, I didn't use the opportunity to take part in *Dry January*. I regretted it, but there didn't seem much point in starting late. Part way through the month I attended a church service where they were encouraging members to do a twenty-one-day fast. Though they were planning a specific food fast, I saw no reason why I shouldn't piggyback on their plan and get a late start on *Dry January*. I could manage twenty-one days.

During the fast, I explored my feelings about drinking. I found via research, the *Reddit Stop Drinking subreddit*. Reddit is an online forum and a subreddit or sub is a forum dedicated to a particular topic. My experience with the forum was the catalyst for me to decide not to start drinking again. I checked in daily and was encouraged to find that many of the members sounded like me. Something happened that was different, and the idea of quitting for good began to form in my mind.

I will issue a caution. *Reddit* can take a bit of getting used to. It is not like Facebook and probably unlike most other social media platforms and forums you might use. Every "sub" has rules, and if you disobey them you will be banned, and sometimes you might get "shadow banned" where you won't know you've been banned and might happily post for a long time before you figure out your posts don't exist to anyone but you. For me, however, the forum was the single most useful resource I found that supported my decision to initially change the way I drank, and ultimately to help me decide not to start again. I learned a lot from the people in the group and their experiences. I also found as in many online forums there were some people I didn't relate to at all and among the helpful posts the occasional rude and intolerant individuals. Reddit is like life—there are corners of it you don't go in without knowing the rules and others you never want to venture into and would be shocked they even exist. The Stop Drinking forum is generally a very supportive and helpful place. I used to check in every morning and see the little badge you can claim with the number of days since you had a drink. It's sad to see how many people are constantly resetting their badge of days without a drink back to zero. Some people continue to go into the Stop Drinking forum for years after they have quit for the continuing support and encouragement. I pop in now and then to see what is new and occasionally to offer encouragement to a new member, but I found that reading about people's drinking relapses made me think about drinking. I rarely think about it and don't want to put it into the forefront of my consciousness every day.

When my first marriage broke up, I read a lot about relationships and devoured novels where the central character was a woman redefining her life. After a while it stopped being my story and my reading material changed. I am not defined by being a drinker or a non-drinker. We are all different and you will find what works for you.

Though I had more than a few moments where I wasn't sure I could move forward in my life without drinking. I began to put plans into place to keep going, along with making sure that I always had alternatives to drink that helped stop any cravings. I also used tapping techniques–Emotional Freedom Techniques (EFT), Visualizations and Affirmations and you can find examples in my videos at

www.youtube.com/trishtaylorcoaching.

When we make a major change in our lives, it is a good idea to keep busy until the change becomes a habit. I used the time to do practical things that kept my mind and body occupied. I read the Marie Kondo book on decluttering, and in the first few weeks after quitting, I did a massive clear out of almost every closet in my house. The physical clearing perfectly complimented the beginnings of my mental and emotional one. I also later did a clearing of my social media feeds and realized that I had toxicity in my life that was not just in my body. I needed to let go of things in my life that triggered me and that included some people I was connected with online. I know that we all have differing views especially when it comes to politics, but there are people who take great delight in pushing our buttons. Toxicity that includes racism or homophobia is not something I am prepared to tolerate. There are also people who should not be allowed near the internet as they are incapable or unwilling to do the research to check their sources before sharing information. The constantly shifting landscape that is social media is one I am still trying to navigate and like most of us I don't always get it right, but at least I do it sober now.

Journaling

I began writing down my thoughts and feelings in a journal after I quit drinking. I am glad I did, it is good to look back and see my growth.

JOURNAL ENTRY, DAY TEN OF NOT DRINKING:

Finally getting my energy back and feeling good. Rethinking the twenty-one-day thing. The more I read the Stop Drinking sub, the more I think I'm ready to say goodbye to alcohol. I can't think of much positives it brings to my life. If I could have just one or two drinks that would be fine but even two leaves me feeling, out of control and useless the next day...Been eating junk but I don't care, one thing at a time. Been running and did a 16-mile bike ride. I'm on the up. It's gonna be okay.

Grateful

love life

again.

I did not have a dramatic insight early on, except for realizing that my emotions were heightened and that this would be a journey of many steps and experiences. I found myself grinding my teeth in my sleep and took steps to deal with that by using some of the self-help techniques I use with my clients.

JOURNAL ENTRY, DAY FIFTY-TWO OF NOT DRINKING:

I didn't realize I had left it so long. Today has been the hardest day so far. It's not that I necessarily wanted to drink. I just had so much anger, that I didn't know what to do with it. I tapped on it which brought out other emotions and ended up crying. All in all, a shitty day. ... Grateful I didn't drink and that I didn't write a nasty gram.

Nights out after you quit might not seem as much fun as before. If your expectation and beliefs are that you cannot have fun without a drink, you will get what you focus on. You might go out and believe everyone drinking is having a great time. The reality is you're focused on what you are missing. You might find it useful to stay away from situations that will leave you feeling uncomfortable or worse, put you in temptation's way. I didn't have a problem with temptation, I just found that some events were a little dull. *Well, then you are not an alcoholic*, shouts the heckler from the cheap seats. And *for the four-hundredth time, I never said I was!* As I've mentioned, I've been in the forums, read thousands of posts, talked to lots of people, and I know that for some the only advice will be–sober people, sober places, be completely selfish, protect your sobriety, and go to a meeting. So are you going to miss your planned vacation? Ditch your sister's wedding or swerve your son's graduation because there might be alcohol involved? You will figure out pretty soon that alcohol is everywhere so, for me, I just learned to get used to the idea and found my own coping mechanisms for dealing with temptation.

There was a time if I saw an image or a video of beer being poured, I felt like I wanted one, I have discovered that when I feel like that it is often because I am thirsty. If I get a craving for a cocktail, it is usually the sugar I want rather than the alcohol. These days rather than being tempted, I am more likely to feel nauseated when I am close to someone holding a glass of wine and am more aware when I can smell it on their breath. This was not how it was in the beginning.

Everyone has a different journey, it is helpful to accept that the way you feel now will change.

JOURNAL ENTRY, SIX MONTHS OF NOT DRINKING:

Just wanted to pop in and say I'm happy things are good and I'm so grateful. Over 6 months since I've had a drink, losing weight, better skin, no morning regrets, no hangovers, minimal arguments. What's not to continue?

... I will succeed, I am succeeding, I will stay the course.

When I first arrived in the United States to begin my new life, I was lonely; I missed my family, my friends, and my job. I was saved by an online forum where there were lots of people like me. I visited daily, sometimes hourly for a few years. I'm grateful for the group and the support I received. I realized that many of the people who frequented the forum regularly would never settle into their life, they were always looking over their shoulder or were planning to return to the UK. Eventually, although it really helped me and I hope that during my time I helped and encouraged others, I stopped visiting regularly. I settled into my new life and became more comfortable. If you quit drinking and identify as someone who doesn't drink you might feel the same about the self-help forums and support groups that you originally need. I have talked to a lot of people who quit drinking. I will say again, one size does not fit all when it comes to the best way forward.

JOURNAL ENTRY, DAY 199 OF NOT DRINKING:

No regrets. It gets better.

- Write a journal entry as if you have quit. What will it say?
- Go look in the mirror. Smile and say, "No thanks, I don't drink." Get used to what that sounds like, without giving an explanation.
- Imagine what you will feel like after not drinking for a week or month a year.

11

EMOTIONS

We drink to feel good. You might not realize that you have been hiding your emotions for a long time, numbing them with a drink. When you finally wake up, you might not like who you are and what you see.

I finally realized I don't need to drink to be an asshole. I can do that all by myself while sober. When the emotions hit, it might shock you to discover that letting yourself feel things can be downright terrifying. I aim to be honest here, and I don't even want to tell you this, but I experienced anxiety after I gave up. I can look back and realize that it has always been there, but it became more magnified after I quit. Alcohol allows you to run and hide from emotions like fear and sadness and also to mask anxiety. After all the alcohol seeped out of my system, it left me with raw emotions and some scary feelings. When we are chasing the next alcohol-induced buzz and then waiting for the hangover to wear off before we do it all again, we rarely have the chance to really *feel*. Well hell! that's the whole point of drinking—so we don't *have* to feel? Or at the very least so we can feel differently. Again, we will all have varying experiences. We don't all drink for the same reasons, and that is why many people find therapy helpful when they quit.

Since I quit, I am often more introspective. I enjoy quiet and time alone and yearn for mountains over parties. I wonder if the anxiety and overthinking is because I spent such a lot of time escaping my thoughts in the past. When my head hits the pillow at night, I love just thinking, planning, pre-dreaming. I so rarely fell asleep in that way when I was drinking, it is so much more preferable than what went before.

I have not stopped feeling anger and some despair, especially when observing injustice and the negative stories in the news. When I felt like this when drinking, I would just drink until the feelings melted away. The next morning, I could often not remember why I felt so bad and the only feelings I had was the hangover and sometimes guilt and shame.

So let's break down what a day might look like for someone who drinks more than is good for them.

Get up, do whatever you need to deal with the hangover.

Wonder if you might have said or done something you should be regretting right now.

Go about your day.

Get angry or triggered about something someone said or did, stay feeling angry or frustrated.

Go home.

Lash out at your significant other or family members.

Quietly get angrier.

Drink, feel better, forget, go to bed, wake up and don't deal with the problem.

And on it goes. We feel angry, sad, frustrated, we drink and feel better for a while and never get to the bottom of what makes us feel this way.

Some days I wake up and it seems like every problem I've ever failed to deal with has come back to hit me in the face, maybe that's why people find the twelve-step program so helpful? because you do get to work through lots of issues with a structured plan to help. When we quit after drinking for a long period of time we may wake to find a lot of debris and unresolved issues stirred up from our past. Learning to live a different life, forgiving ourselves and moving forward can be painful. This is why I suggest you get help whether it's in the form of therapy or a program that works for you.

JOURNAL ENTRY, DAY 430 OF NOT DRINKING:

Just checking in to say that I am no longer really counting. I have no real desire to drink, occasionally look at a beer or wine and it looks inviting but no real urge. Busy with other things, a few aches and pains. My skin is looking better. Dealing with emotions is hard. I am such a child when it comes to handling stuff that upsets me and yet. I am grateful.

PAUSE AND REFLECT:

- Which emotions do you attempt to block with alcohol?
- How has this helped you?
- How has it hurt you?
- What is your strategy for dealing with these emotions without having a drink?

12

ARE YOU READY TO QUIT?

I have recently been following discussions online about Sober October—an annual quit drinking project that encourages participants to quit drinking for one month and donate money saved to a designated charitable cause. Much of the talk on social media is around the impossibility of going for a whole month without a drink. If you feel like this, be encouraged, because virtually everyone does at the beginning and many people do continue to be alcohol-free for months and even years.

Quitting is a process, a journey. It might be cliché, but it really helps to take that one-day-at-a-time approach to staying away from alcohol. If you try and you fail, you can start again, and you might learn what led you to drink again. Hopefully, you will be stronger next time.

There are three things worth considering:

1. Why you drink
2. Where and when you drink
3. How you drink

Why You Drink

We have briefly touched on the why. If you want to delve into this further, I would encourage you to consider therapy or some other form of help. Many people find it helpful to learn if there is a root cause to their reasons for drinking. Remember, we drink because we want to change our *state*—the way we feel. You might have done that in the beginning but have now developed a habit. If you have a deep-seated root cause and don't uncover it, you could find yourself later replacing alcohol with a different drug or state-inducing activity.

Where and When You Drink

If you associated your habit with a place or events, you might need to change your routine. If you always drank during specific activities such as when you went bowling, played cards or went to a friend's house, it is possible you will feel cheated if you don't drink when you next go, or it may be too much of a temptation. There are things I no longer have any desire to do and were only tolerable if I was half drunk—did I mention baby showers already? Other activities seemed like such fun when I drank that I don't want to do them anymore and risk being disappointed. You know yourself, and you must test things and see what works.

How You Drink

Do you drink alone? In secret? With food? To celebrate? To commiserate? It is worth considering all the reasons and writing them down.

Buy yourself a beautiful journal and regularly write about your feelings. It will help you identify what makes you more likely to want to drink. Discovering patterns and triggers will be helpful. Admit your feelings and recognize your emotions, as we have discussed this can be a huge part of your journey.

Write a letter to yourself. I found this really helpful. When we drink and have an unhealthy relationship with it, we can be in denial. After we have done the stupid thing, got a DUI, offended someone, lost our wallet, we might temporarily stop drinking. When the shame and guilt wear off, it is easy to convince ourselves that we don't have a problem and start drinking again, only to be back where we started in no time. In my letter, I reminded myself of the things I had said, felt, done, and contemplated. I laid it all out so it was there in black and white.

See Chapter 17 for suggestions on how to write the letter.

Choose a Time ... or Don't

I quit drinking in January and still had drinks left over from Christmas. A friend had bought me a bottle of champagne in a beautiful decorative bottle. I had saved it to open on a special occasion. As the break from drinking was not meant to be permanent, I did not have an advance plan to finish all of my favorite items in our liquor cabinet and therefore it was not in my mind to consume the contents of the fancy bottle before I quit. As the twenty-one days of the fast rolled on and I had been reading, thinking, and meditating on the idea of not restarting drinking, the fancy bottle tempted me, not because I was desperate to drink the contents, but because I had a fear of missing out. What if the inside of the bottle was as lovely as the outside? What if I offended my friend who bought me the gift? Couldn't I drink the champagne and go back to quitting afterward? It was all stupid thinking, and I know that now just as I knew it then.

If you quit drinking—whether you believe it is an addiction, a disease or a bad habit—the urge to drink takes time to let go of. It can take even longer for you to feel comfortable with the idea of not drinking long term. Just like quitting anything that you crave or are addicted to, a little can make you want more, and many people believe that it gets harder to quit with each time you fail and try again. Not to say that you won't be able to, but it helps to understand why those who quit celebrate their sober days, weeks, and years. It is fragile and held tightly because that one drink can have you back to where you started, or even further back and spiraling down. So the next time my friend came around, I made sure she was part of a group who drank the champagne. By that time I was fully committed to staying alcohol-free.

This might be just the beginning for you. You might read this, toss it aside, and decide that you are happy as you are. You don't smoke, you eat well, so you are just going to keep on drinking. We have to have some vices, right? Only you know if that is the correct way forward. Drinking is sometimes fun in the moment yet rarely leaves us with anything positive. Some people end up with:

Unplanned pregnancies

Sexually transmitted diseases

Missing credit cards

Lost jewelry

Harsh words that cannot be taken back

Drunk driving convictions

A night in a jail cell

Seriously injured

Dead

Although I have only experienced one of the above—guess, I dare you! Okay it's lost jewelry! I have definitely had plenty of the other less risky legacies of a drunken night. A hangover, for instance. I searched everywhere for the perfect hangover cure to finally discover not drinking worked really well.

I asked a family member who is a police officer what percentage of his calls are alcohol-related. He shrugged his shoulders and said, "most of them," then thought a little further and clarified that alcohol and drugs are a factor in many of the problems he deals with. People argue over insignificant events that may not escalate if all parties were sober. That's the problem with alcohol—it makes you dumb. I've had a few moments of creativity when floating on a cloud of ethanol, but mostly I've said and done things that in the clear light of day are stupid and cringeworthy.

Alcohol Is a Drug

Some people like to frame alcohol as a poison. It is a toxin, which is a poison. Withdrawal from alcohol must be handled carefully because it can be fatal. Because alcohol is legal, it seems the only way we can talk about it as a problem is by defining problem drinkers as alcoholics. But surely there is something between responsible drinking and what many consider a disease.

I don't believe I have or ever have had a disease. I believe I moved from drinking socially to drinking somewhat irresponsibly to not being sure I could stop to needing it too much to believing I had a problem. Your experience might be different. I want to reach that large group of people who are still wondering if they drink too much, if they can stop, and if they will have to quit for good.

If, while reading this book, you have decided that your relationship with alcohol is healthy then I am happy for you. If you are reading and are still not sure, it is sometimes useful to observe other people, not those who you see who drink and fall over, but those who you believe have a healthy relationship with their drinking. It wasn't until I saw people who could open a bottle of wine, have a glass, and leave it on the counter that I realized I was different. That would never be still sitting there three days later. Or if I went to a hotel and had to scope out where I could get a bottle of wine for the room before I had decided what I was going to eat. It feels pretty awkward sharing this. I don't want people to think, *There goes Trish. She's a bit of an 'alchy.* Most of what I am sharing went on in my head. My close friends have witnessed my slurred speech and drunken silliness. In the UK, it was almost a badge of honor. It's not who I want to be any more.

Will I drink again? Not today. Probably not tomorrow. I don't really like the smell of alcohol anymore. But I won't say never because that's a pressure I am not prepared to put on myself. I encourage you to consider my disclaimer and advice and then to take a break from drinking. Look at the world with a set of clear eyes. Imagine what it might feel like to wake up after a night out without a hangover.

PAUSE AND REFLECT:

- If you want to quit drinking and feel you are not ready, what do you need to do to be ready?
- When you think about quitting, what does it look like? What is the location? Who are you with?
- Imagine a powerful, positive, happy version of you that doesn't include drinking alcohol. Make the picture in your mind big, vivid, and bright. Add sounds and feelings to make it a powerful visualization.

YOU THINK YOU MIGHT BE READY TO DRINK AGAIN

Yes, it's the big one. Why can everyone else drink normally and I can't? After about a year of not drinking, a period of time that had previously seemed impossible. I got used to not drinking. I patted myself on the back and realized I could actually do this thing. I began to toy with the idea of moderation. Having proved that I could abstain from drinking, I starting to wonder if I could just enjoy one drink on my birthday. Birthdays have always been the one day of the year for me where I can do what I want. Looking back, they seem almost magical. I missed the sparkle that alcohol added to those types of occasions where it was so often central.

So what if I drank but only on my birthday and Christmas? Christmas was a time that did not feel special without a glass of something festive in my hand, and there were always so many yummy Christmas drinks that also included cream and chocolate. Come to think of it, I should probably just add New Year's and Christmas Eve. They're all right there together. And I guess I should include the times when I go back to England because it's a bit weird not drinking when I go back, and everyone's will start to ask questions. I bet you're seeing where this is headed. Before long there would be more special occasions than normal days, which would eventually lead me back to drinking regularly. So I decided not to bother with the moderation idea. I read lots of accounts of other people going down the same route and soon going back to drinking on a regular basis, often becoming heavier drinkers than when they started. I didn't want that to happen. It had taken me years to decide to quit and it seemed a waste to go back and mess with moderation.

The problem with moderation is that you have to put in such a lot of effort to make it work. If you are reading this, you probably have already tried to limit how much you drink and failed.

So this moderation plan, it goes something like this.

I will have just one, OK, maybe two drinks, once a week. But one gets you going, gives you a taste, gets the desire stirred up. One drink is foreplay. You can't do that because you are just being a drink tease. So maybe three, no more than once a month, only on your birthday, when someone else is there, you will put a reminder on your phone and after three, you are cut off. But three is the danger zone. Three is the road to five and the hangover, all the arguments, the regret, and in no time at all, you're back to where you started. That's why I gave up on the idea of moderation. In time I enjoyed the simplicity of saying, "No, I don't drink." I enjoyed not having to plan, plot, and count, hoping against hope I didn't lose my will and end up regretting my decision.

I am not saying I will never drink again. Never is a long time. I sometimes think of the situations and scenarios where I might just go for it and drink again. My little lizard brain still pops up every now and again and tempts me, so I give myself room for flexibility. There are a few situations where I have promised myself I can drink if I feel the need.

If someone close to me dies. My dad passed, and I managed to get through that without drinking. In all honesty, it wouldn't have helped.

If I develop a terminal illness. Again, it's unlikely that I would choose to further damage my health.

If there is an apocalypse, and I am one of the last people on earth and come across a liquor store.

If...

How ridiculous is this conversation? That's why, my dear reader, people say I'm not drinking *today*. If you think of every scenario that might justify a drink, the list is endless and not at all helpful. (Though I like to play the game now and then.)

My celebrations are different now. They have sometimes been a disappointment because getting drunk requires no creativity. When we don't rely solely on alcohol for fun, we have to plan rather than just expect to have an amazing time. We may have to think a little harder to find alternatives. My fortieth birthday was one of the most wonderful celebrations I have ever had, and I went home totally sober. I organized a fundraiser for Amnesty International and it included bands, a chess challenge, and salsa dancing. I was so busy running around, organizing activities and catching up with friends, I didn't have time to drink.

The world can be a very scary place and vividly terrifying without the blurriness, the sharp edges exposed. I'm not saying it will be easy. Some days when I feel like a failure, when I accept that some of my dreams haven't yet come true, I look in the mirror and say, "But I did give up drinking."

No Alcohol Necessary

This is when I find it helpful to consider all the wonderful things I like that are perfect just the way they are. So many experiences in this life can be amazing without a drink, and most of them can be done without too much effort or expense. Here are a few:

Eating great food

Walking on the beach

Listening to an orchestra

Laughing at hilarious comedy

Watching a great movie

Hugging or lovemaking

Cooking

Climbing a mountain

Ice cream

Rollercoasters

Reading

Sitting around a campfire or fire pit

I'm sure you can think of many more juicy things you prefer that have an intoxication of their own. There are so many activities that are perfect as they are with a clear head. We have become convinced that we need a drink to make everything better. Experiences can be perfect exactly as they are unadulterated, pure and filled with clarity. When I climbed the mountains in the Himalayas, we were not allowed alcohol on the ascent as it could mask the symptoms of altitude sickness. We had a beer at the top, and though it was enjoyable, it was unmemorable compared to the views of some of the world's tallest mountains, a far superior buzz than an alcoholic one.

PAUSE AND REFLECT:

- Think of a time when you successfully moderated your drinking.
- Think of something that you love doing alone that doesn't include alcohol.
- List your favorite shared activities that are best done sober.

14

HABITS, TEMPTATION, AND YOUR
FUTURE RELATIONSHIP WITH
ALCOHOL

L et's say you decide to quit. What now? If you have tried and failed several times or you know it is going to be a struggle, then you need a plan. A plan is always good when you start something because it sets you up for success. Remember, if you are a heavy drinker who has had problems in the past, this is not something you should do alone.

There are physical, emotional and mental changes happening, and everyone is different. If you decide to follow an established program, there is a system already in place for you. If, like many of my readers, you are a social drinker who has decided to quit, you will still need a plan.

When we have had a habit for a long time, it is natural to want to replace it with something else. Drinking gives you a feeling, a buzz, a taste, and something to put in your hand. After initially thinking I could never enjoy my hobby of long baths while drinking a glass of my favorite wine, I discovered the drink that I liked while soaking in the bath could be a fizzy drink, craft soda, or even an ice-cold glass of water. It was not the alcohol that made the experience pleasurable, it was the bath I enjoyed, the feeling of relaxation. I could replicate this feeling with luxurious soaps, fragrant bath oils, and a cold glass of soda water with natural flavors. It did not even have any calories!

You might find yourself substituting things—some are okay and some are not.

Doughnuts, ice cream, fizzy water, baked kale, whatever floats your boat that you put in your mouth is okay, especially in the short term. It becomes risky if you find yourself searching for a replacement drug. Alcohol has been filling a hole in your life for some time and you may unconsciously search for something to fill its place.

Some people are triggered by even tiny amounts of alcohol and cannot be around it at all. Since I have quit drinking there has always been alcohol in the house. I have not knowingly or purposefully consumed food with alcohol. Initially, I avoided anything that made me want to drink. Some things you might find a problem with and others you might not.

Non-Alcoholic Beer

A huge debate surrounds non-alcoholic beer. I have seen people attack others who drink an occasional non-alcoholic beer. Let me give you my take on it. If you like the taste of NA beer and know that an occasional bottle will not cause you to go out and have the real stuff, that is up to you.

On a recent vacation, we were given drinks vouchers for the hotel bar. I got into the vacation mode by having an NA beer. It was OK, and I felt it added to the holiday mood. When I came home, I bought a pack so I could have one when I wanted. After getting half-way down a bottle, I realized it wasn't making me feel good like the first beer would, and it didn't particularly taste great. Mostly it left me wanting something else—a real beer. So ask yourself why you really want that NA beer? Is it giving you what you want? If it leaves you unfulfilled and searching for the buzz that it doesn't deliver, you might want to leave it alone. I went back to having other types of fizzy drinks. I know they are not necessarily good for us, but a nice cold glass of sparkling ginger ale can be a delight at the end of a hard day. It doesn't get you drunk, but the act of drinking something cold and fizzy has a buzz of its own.

You will find similar debates about other foods that might include traces of alcohol. These include:

- Fermented drinks such as Kombucha contain small amounts of alcohol. There are also hard kombuchas, so be sure to check labels before you buy or consume.
- Mouthwash is often alcohol based.
- Communion wine-though it is often grape juice. When I went to Church in the UK it was usually actual fermented wine and some churches in the US also use real wine.
- Alcohol flavored desserts can have quite a lot of alcohol in them. I once had a liquor-soaked crepe in France that had me quite buzzed.
- Food cooked with alcohol, the alcohol isn't all burned off in the cooking process as people often think.
- Chocolate liqueurs. In the states, it's often fake alcohol (really, what's the point?) whereas in Europe it's a small shot of alcohol. We used to love them as kids. Maybe that's where it all started.

The main question is: Does it trigger you to want to drink? If you are not sure, you might be better steering clear of anything that could put you in the danger zone.

Warnings can be helpful, but we are not a one-size-fits-all society. When I quit smoking and relapsed, I would wander out in the middle of the night to find a gas station, so I could smoke—usually when I had been drinking. If the craving is strong and overpowering, it might not matter if there is alcohol in the house or not.

Most people don't go out intending to drink and drive. It happens gradually. After the first drink, they begin to lose self-control. Then comes the belief they are safe to drive. The arrogance that often comes with alcohol in the system means it is often difficult, if not damn near impossible, to talk someone out of driving if they are adamant. I remember being at a wedding, and a man I knew, who it turned out was an idiot in other areas of his life too, insisted he was okay to drive though he was "pissed as a fart," as we would say. We managed to convince him not to drive, at some point taking his keys from him. He later assured us he wouldn't drive and was given a bed for the night. He secretly returned to his vehicle and drove home in spite of the warnings. He didn't hurt anyone that night. Someone else I know of did take a life and lost his family's home in the process. There are plenty of other stories of misery caused by those who thought they could handle their drink and couldn't. But you didn't come here for that. You don't need scaring straight, you need to decide whether to stop drinking. Should you quit? Should you moderate or just cross your fingers and hope all will be okay? Doesn't sound like much of a plan, does it?

I am fairly self-aware regarding drinking and the potential risk of looking to for a replacement, but it caught me off guard when I took a prescription painkiller that had a side effect of making me feel really good. It was legally prescribed, and I had taken it for genuine pain, but the euphoric feeling that came with it was too enjoyable and left me wanting more. No wonder there is an opioid epidemic when these drugs that can be acquired fairly easily create such a feeling. The next time I wanted to take one, I asked myself if the pain was that bad, or if I could use something safer and non-addictive such as Tylenol. I flushed what was left of my prescription. As you move closer to making your decision, remember it is possible you might find other drugs—and their side effects—just as tempting as alcohol.

Other substances I have heard people be tempted by include:

Laughing gas at the dentist.

A smoke of someone's joint.

Or even a cigarette.

Only you can know if these temptations will lead you down a dangerous path. Is it worth the risk?

PAUSE AND REFLECT:

- What will you need to avoid when you first quit drinking?
- What plans will you put in place to make sure you have options and alternatives?
- What will it feel like when you avoid temptation and realize you no longer need alcohol to feel good?

15

SWEET RELIEF: MILESTONES AND REWARDS

If you decide to quit, you might find it useful to have a stock of alternatives to alcohol on hand. After quitting drinking some people crave sugar so this chapter includes ideas to show you that drinking something other than alcohol does not have to be boring. I allowed myself to have what I wanted in the early days even if it was often sweet.

When I was out for dinner recently and asked the server if they had any interesting soft drinks, I got the dismissive "Coke products" answer. I have nothing against Coke or Sprite, yet they are not my preferred option with dinner. I have learned not to accept the first answer and politely push back. Then our server realized she had a whole bar at her disposal and went off to find me a ginger beer. Most restaurants have a bar that along with all of the alcohol we are avoiding can provide.

Craft sodas

Tonic water

Orange juice

Apple juice

Tomato juice

Pineapple juice

Blackcurrant

Lemonade

Root beer

Lime and soda—if you are a Brit, you will have probably drunk this in a bar at some point when you were trying to save money or just wanted a refreshing alternative to a regular soft drink. Bars in the UK will normally charge a nominal amount to add a couple of shots of lime juice to a club soda. Not always as inexpensive in the US when I was charged the price of a regular soda.

You could also enjoy hot chocolate, fruit and herbal teas, and numerous *mocktails*. You might also discover that if you are in a bar with friends and you order a soda, you will get the designated-driver free drink as I did recently. Score!

Drinking at Home

My favorite drinks to enjoy at home when I'm not drinking hot tea or coffee include craft sodas or any fruit drink with a slice of lime and topped off with club soda. One of my favorite alcoholic drinks was an elderflower liquor. I discovered you can buy an elderflower cordial or soda that satisfies my elderflower craving without the alcohol. In the states, it is a little harder to find—check out health food stores or World Market. In the UK, there are lots of different versions and all taste delicious topped up with soda water. What the United States has that the UK doesn't at the time of writing is subtly and naturally fruit-flavored soda water. It is evenly loved and hated. It is definitely not to be confused with a regular soda, and the taste is too subtle for some people, but it has zero calories or artificial sweeteners, so it works for me. For some of us, that fizz at the back of the throat is enough to satisfy a craving that in the past only an alcoholic drink could fulfill.

Here are other non-alcoholic drink ideas for experimenting at home. Some of them require a blender. Don't have one? Maybe you can buy one with the money you save by not buying booze!

Watermelon Spritz

Blend ripe watermelon with crushed ice top up with soda add a slice of lime or lemon.

Smoothies

Blend your favorite fruits and veggies together for a healthy and filling alternative to drinking.

Frozen fruit

I found frozen cherries in particular to be a wonderful craving buster as well as just about any fruit. Grapes, pineapple and strawberries and covered in melted chocolate–even better.

Ice Cream

I ate a LOT of ice cream in the early days and can get through a tub by eating a bowl or two every day until it was gone. I found that buying ice cream cones helped me to limit myself to one scoop. There are so many amazing flavors available. I can spend as much time looking at the ice cream freezer as I did in the wine aisle.

Bake

Even if you are not a regular baker, l find baking something sweet and delicious fills the house with lovely smells and you end up with a cake, pie or treat.

Dehydrate something

We recently discovered the joys of dehydrating and now can spend an evening thinly slicing fruit and vegetables ready for the dehydrator. If that sounds boring well wait until you taste the results. Mango and watermelon slices are their own form of chewy deliciousness and I crave them like I used to want wine.

Savory Treats

If you prefer savory to sweet treats, chop up veggies and find a tasty dip or you can even experiment by making your own dips, salsa, hummus or guacamole.

Craving Busters

When we get any kind of craving it helps to put some distance between us and the thing we crave. Just a few minutes of an activity can take our mind of it and shift our focus.

Here are suggestions of activities that will stop you thinking about drinking:

- Do a few pushups or any physical exercise
- Sing a song
- Drink water
- Take out the trash
- Make a phone call
- Delete or organize emails
- Brush your teeth
- Say positive affirmations
- Breathe and pause
- Water your plants
- Dust your bookshelf
- Clean out the fridge
- Check the use by dates on canned food
- Walk your dog

Rewards

I am very motivated by reward, and I find that it is much more effective than punishment. Making any big change in your life is worthy of a reward, so if you hit a big number in your days without a drink, make sure to mark it and celebrate. There are lots of things you can do that don't involve drinking. I like to do something relaxing to celebrate, such as a facial—men, you can enjoy these too. I also have been known to go to the movies alone, buy new clothes, or take an afternoon off. Reading fiction is also a great escape or maybe you prefer to binge watch a show on Netflix. I have recently rewarded myself by having personal fitness sessions. I am more invested than ever in my health and I'm excited to see what my body is capable of.

PAUSE AND REFLECT:

- If you were to quit. What alternatives would be helpful to have in the house to make sure you don't get tempted?
- What activity might help you with cravings?
- What do you look forward to enjoying instead of alcohol?

16

HELPFUL RESOURCES FOR QUITTING DRINKING

I mentioned that when we drink, we are doing it because we want to change our state. Here are some helpful activities that might help to distract you if you are working through a craving or dealing with temptation.

MEDITATION:

Get used to being still. There are numerous ways to meditate, allow yourself to find what works for you.

EXERCISE:

I know some people quit drinking and become obsessed with body building or running. You don't have to take it to that extreme but if as many people do, you begin to see weight drop off and feel stronger, you may decide that you want to look after your body and become more health conscious.

TAPPING TECHNIQUES:

Check out my videos on how to use therapeutic tapping for cravings at YouTube.com/trishtaylorcoaching

PEOPLE YOU KNOW AND TRUST:

If you know someone who you trust that has already quit drinking they could be a really good resource.

ONLINE EVENTS

If you quit at a time of year like *Dry January* or *Sober October* you will find a lot of online support. Though it is aimed at people who are taking a break from drinking rather than those who have identified as having a problem there are still good resources available.

Below I have listed resources that could be useful though they are not necessarily tried and tested by me personally. The group I used is the *Stop Drinking Forum* on Reddit. If you want to do support online rather than in person this is a good place to start. If you are unfamiliar with *Reddit,* I recommend you learn the etiquette before diving in. You will find an up to date guide if you search *How to Use Reddit.*

RESOURCES AND SUPPORT GROUPS

This is not an exhaustive list. I am sure there are many other groups, forums, books, and resources that you will find helpful.

STOP DRINKING - REDDIT FORUM

https://www.reddit.com/r/stopdrinking/

DRY JANUARY AND BEYOND:

https://www.alcoholconcern.org.uk/dry-january

Great resources including an app - not just for January.

SAMHSA

(Substance Abuse and Mental Health Services Administration)

https://www.samhsa.gov/find-help/national-helpline

National helpline in the US.

RETHINKING DRINKING

https://www.rethinkingdrinking.niaaa.nih.gov

Includes calculators and alcohol counts for those who find them helpful.

HAMS

http://hams.cc

Harm Reduction for Alcohol: Support for safer drinking, reduced drinking, or quitting

HAMS is a peer-led and free-of-charge support and informational group for anyone who wants to change their drinking habits for the better.

SMART RECOVERY

https://www.smartrecovery.org

Offers meetings in the United States, Canada, Australia, Denmark,

Ireland and the UK as well as many other countries around the world. Find a meeting in your area, or attend an online meeting.

LIFERING

https://lifering.org

Secular based recovery. Meetings in USA and Canada and other selected countries.

RATIONAL RECOVERY

https://rational.org

The opposite of a treatment program and incompatible with treatment groups and recovery groups.

ALCOHOLICS ANONYMOUS (AA)

https://www.aa.org

Alcoholics Anonymous (AA) is an international mutual aid fellowship whose stated purpose is to enable its members to stay sober and help other alcoholics achieve sobriety.

MODERATION MANAGEMENT

https://www.moderation.org

Is a lay led non-profit dedicated to reducing the harm caused by the abuse of alcohol.

WOMEN FOR SOBRIETY, INC

An Organization of Women, For Women

https://womenforsobriety.org

A non-profit organization dedicated to helping women discover a happy new life in recovery from Substance Use Disorders.

PAUSE AND REFLECT:

- What resources do you plan to use?
- What will you have for a support system?
- Who in your life will you feel comfortable to go to for support?

17

A LETTER TO MYSELF

W hen I finally decided that I probably wouldn't drink again, I wrote a letter so I would remember the reasons why I had made the decision. At the time, I really did not want anyone else to read it, but I wanted it to be there as a reminder. I knew the day might come when I decided that I was ready to drink again. I password protected the letter so it was for my eyes only.

This letter is a reminder for when you forget why you made your decision. For those days when you're on the edge. As the days roll forward and you need encouragement, you can read your own words. Write it down before you forget, before the denial kicks in. I also wrote messages or had conversations with a few people close to me, not as any kind of confession, just laying out that I was taking a break from drinking, citing the reasons why and asking for support and encouragement rather than questions and judgments.

The reason many people say *I'm never drinking again* after a terrible hangover or embarrassing incident and then drink again is that they forget how bad it was. A painful and difficult experience can make us stop what we're doing for a while and re-evaluate, yet that feeling will usually fade in time.

I was once caught speeding. The car I was driving, my American boyfriend (now husband), told me was a *hooptie or* an *old banger* in the UK. The cop who pulled me over commented, rather disparagingly, that he was surprised my car even managed to reach the speed I was going, but he gave me the ticket despite his doubts about my car's performance. When I visited the police station to pay my fine, I told the desk sergeant that I now was probably driving everyone mad going under the speed limit. "Yeah, it will slow you down for a bit," he said, clearly indicating that he didn't believe it would slow me down for long. In most cases, when we're penalized for doing something wrong, we eventually return to our bad habits.

The hangover from hell, the embarrassing conversation, even broken relationships can be forgotten when the desire to drink takes over. There has to be a reason why people with six DUIs will get behind the wheel to make it seven. So a carefully thought out letter listing the reasons why it's a good time to quit might be helpful and won't do any harm. You don't have to share it with anyone else. I suggest keeping it in a safe place. Sometimes we have to be careful because we might have an employer or a family member who judges us. This is something just for you. If you do quit, you might also find it helpful to write down all the reasons you are glad you quit.

A Letter to Myself (This is a guide. Amend it so that it will work for you!)

Dear Trish,

I am guessing you have done pretty well so far and have gone for x months without drinking, that is a great achievement and I am very proud of you. Remember when you never believed you would get to this stage?

You wanted to wake up with a clear head, to be able to remember what you said and did and to feel better about yourself. You also wanted to be stronger and fitter and no longer have that worry that you might be damaging your liver.

I knew this day would come where you would become confident in your abilities to drink again and to do it in "moderation," look in the mirror and ask yourself, do I ever do things in moderation?

I know you believe you are thinking about drinking differently than most people who have a problem, that is what you are saying right? You have resisted drink, never been tempted by the drinks at home, in the bar, at dinner, at your friend's wedding. You have managed to resist all of that, so you have pretty much proved you don't have a problem. If you had a problem, it's gone now. And it's not like you are planning on going on a bender. You just want to enjoy that special occasion that's coming up with a glass of fizz, have a beer on vacation or whatever specially designated occasion you are planning. The fact that you have found this letter and are reading it means that you are not totally set in your plan, yet, so I want to encourage you to read to the end and remember why you quit.

Before you decide to do anything, I want you to remember the days you woke up and said:

I'm never drinking again

I wish I could stop drinking

I am tired of feeling like this

Remember the people you hurt, upset or offended.

Your bank balance

Your growth

Your achievement

Your badge or counter that tells you how many days since you quit

Think about the early days, how you felt and how hard it was

Your health

Your weight

Your relationships

All the things that have improved since you stopped drinking

I want you to especially remember these reasons:

```



```

(*This is where you would write your reasons*)

(Be HONEST. Write the serious things that you regret)

I know it's hard to read. Yet, you wrote this for a reason.

I hope this is enough to convince you to stick with the plan, until the next time.

Trish

WRITING YOUR LETTER

Even if you can't face writing down every detail of a significant incident in your past, make sure that you write something that will remind you of what happened. Here are some prompts and guidelines to help you in writing your letter:

I want to achieve

I want to change

The worst thing I did while drinking was

The worst thing I felt while drinking was

The worst thing I remember saying while drinking was

I once woke up and realized that

I once forgot to

The way she looked at me when

When he told me that

When I jeopardized

That thing that no one knows except you - *give it a code word if you don't want to put it in writing*

Write this letter when you decide to quit, write another when you hit a milestone, write one on your birthday, at Christmas, and recognize your feelings regularly. But do make sure that you write one when you have made the life-changing decision to quit. Though you can type it, it is helpful to write from your heart without editing.

18

WORKBOOK - YOUR ACTION PLAN

Here is a list of the questions and action items from each chapter. As you write the answers to each question you will have the beginnings of a plan for when you are ready to quit.

Imagine there was a book about your drinking: How would it begin?

What would be the central theme?

How would you like it to end?

When and where did your drinking years start?

Where and when did your drinking years start?

When did they change?

What significant event if any, happened?

What was your worst hangover?

What did you lose or gain from this hangover?

ACTION: Think of an event that you didn't enjoy because you had a hangover. Picture how it might have been without it?

When you think about your drinking, what is the first thing that springs to mind when answering this question? *I would find it hard to quit drinking because of* ... (Think about people and situations.)

What other reasons or justifications are holding you back from quitting?

ACTION: Think about the drinkers you admire. Do you believe you know the full story behind their drinking?

Think of a time when you have had strong regrets about drinking. What happened?

Think of a time when you put yourself or someone else at risk with your drinking. What could have happened?

Have you ever lost an evening because of drinking or been unable to remember how you behaved? What did that feel like?

What bargains have you made? Which worked?

Do you bargain with other substances or habits? Why or why not?

Is your drinking a problem?

Has your behavior around drinking ever hurt anyone?

How did that feel?

What were the consequences?

ACTION: If you were to know, on a scale of 1 to 10 how much of a problem is it? (1 being no problem at all and 10 being the worst it could possibly be.) Why not write that number down somewhere? You don't have to tell anyone else or make a decision. Just answer the question honestly and give it a number.

List three ways that your life might be better without alcohol in it?

What are some things that alcohol keeps you from accomplishing?

Who in your life would be overjoyed if you stopped drinking?

ACTION: Think of a time when you have spent money on alcohol that you couldn't afford?

Work out the following: How much your drinks cost. Calculate and average how much you drink in a week, month and year. Get a figure.

Think of a bucket list item that you could spend that money on. What would it be?

What worries do you have around quitting?

What kinds of situations worry you the most?

If you quit, who are you worried about telling?

Who will you look forward to telling?

Write a journal entry as if you have quit. What will it say?

ACTION: Go look in the mirror. Smile and say,

"No thanks, I don't drink." Get used to what that sounds like, without giving an explanation.

ACTION: Imagine what you will feel like after not drinking for a week, a month, a year.

. . .

Which emotions do you attempt to block with alcohol?

How has this helped you?

How has it hurt you?

What is your strategy for dealing with these emotions without having a drink?

If you want to quit drinking and feel you are not ready, what do you need to do to be ready?

When you think about quitting, what does it look like? What is the location? Who are you with?

ACTION: Imagine a powerful, positive, happy version of you that doesn't include drinking alcohol. Make the picture in your mind big, vivid and bright. Add sounds and feelings to make it a powerful visualization.

Think of a time when you successfully moderated your drinking.

Think of something that you love doing alone that doesn't include alcohol.

```
┌─────────────────────────────────────────────────────────┐
│                                                         │
│                                                         │
│                                                         │
│                                                         │
│                                                         │
└─────────────────────────────────────────────────────────┘
```

List your favorite shared activities that are best done sober.

```
┌─────────────────────────────────────────────────────────┐
│                                                         │
│                                                         │
│                                                         │
│                                                         │
│                                                         │
│                                                         │
└─────────────────────────────────────────────────────────┘
```

What will you need to avoid when you first quit drinking?

```
┌─────────────────────────────────────────────────────────┐
│                                                         │
│                                                         │
│                                                         │
│                                                         │
│                                                         │
│                                                         │
└─────────────────────────────────────────────────────────┘
```

What plans will you put in place to make sure you have options and alternatives?

```
┌─────────────────────────────────────────────────────────┐
│                                                         │
│                                                         │
│                                                         │
│                                                         │
│                                                         │
└─────────────────────────────────────────────────────────┘
```

What will it feel like when you avoid temptation and realize you no longer need alcohol to feel good?

If you were to quit. What alternatives would be helpful to have in the house to make sure that you don't get tempted?

What activity might help you with cravings?

What do you look forward to enjoying instead of alcohol?

What resources do you plan to use?

What will you have for a support system?

Who in your life will you feel comfortable to go to for support?

ACTION: Write Your Letter to Yourself

CLOSING THOUGHTS

If you have come this far and you are ready to consider quitting drinking, even though it may not be easy, I am excited for you. There is a part of your life that is only just beginning, one that can be better than you imagined.

There will be days where you will believe that you need a drink. You might experience the crappy day, the horrible boss, the inconsiderate partner, the bratty child, the unfair decision, the painful diagnosis, the tragic loss, the debilitating fear, the shocking pain, the emptiness, the failure. You will get through this.

You will realize that hangovers are not an obligatory part of life and neither are shame or guilt. You will learn that life can be glorious in its unadulterated beauty, that it has everything you need without the dullness, without the edges obscured.

If you want to quit drinking and are ready, I wish you well. I hope this book will lead you in the direction you need to go.

If you decide to continue drinking, please drink responsibly and be mindful of those in your life who may be affected by your drinking.

Don't be tempted to drink and drive and be open and come back to this book or others like it. Continue to regularly examine your relationship to alcohol as it might change.

I'm not drinking today. I have no plans to drink again. If you decide to join me, let me know how it goes.

Trish

Please remember my disclaimer regarding quitting alcohol. Check with your doctor before making a change.

BOOK SUGGESTIONS

Books I or others have found helpful or that I have referenced in this book:

Dry: A Memoir by Augusten Burroughs

Recovery: Freedom from Our Addictions by Russell Brand

Kick the Drink!... Easily by Jason Vale

The Life-Changing Magic of Tidying Up by Marie Kondo

The Power of Habit by Charles Duhigg

Meditation for Fidgety Skeptics by Dan Harris

The Power of your Subconscious Mind by Joseph Murphy

The Four Agreements by Don Miguel Ruiz

The Untethered Soul: The Journey Beyond Self by Michael A Singer

This Naked Mind by Annie Grace

Quit Drinking Without Willpower by Allen Carr

ABOUT THE AUTHOR

Trish Taylor is the author of *Why Am I Scared?: Face Your Fears and Learn to Let Them Go*. And co-author of *Respect in the Workplace: You have to give it to get it*. Her newest self-help book *Yes! You Are Good Enough* is available now.

Trish is an Author and Speaker. A Master Practitioner and Trainer of Neuro-Linguistic Programming (NLP), Master Practitioner of Mental Emotional Release and Practitioner in Advanced Thought Field Therapy.

She has helped clients gain success with: weight loss, confidence, quitting smoking and drinking, fear of flying, test anxiety and healing of family relationships.

Trish lived happily in England until a salsa dance led to a chance encounter with an American who literally swept her off her feet. She left her job of 14 years as a career counselor and side business as a Jazz Singer and moved to the United States in 2005.

Trish currently lives in Florida with her husband.

Made in the USA
Monee, IL
28 September 2020

43441878R00083